A Seed In The Fruit Of Palestine
a collection of short essays
(Some previously published)

Mike Odetalla

Copyright © 2024 Mike Odetalla

All rights reserved. No part of this publication may be reproduced, stored, or transmitted in any form or by any means, electronic, mechanical, photocopying, recording, scanning, or otherwise, without written permission from the publisher. It is illegal to copy this book, post it to a website, or distribute it by any other means without permission.

ISBN: 9798880447619

Cover design images: Depositphotos with licnese to use commercially

Table of Contents

Dedication 5
Memories 7
First Love 9
Today's Dinner 15
Desecrating the memory of Babe Ruth 19
Alfi laila wa laila 23
The Olive Harvest 27
Love and Refugees 31
"The Israeli Experience" 33
Benny Morris and Ethnic Cleansing 35
"Thanking" Sharon 39
Olive trees, Oum Kulthoum, and Jasmine Blossoms 47
Blocking Out the Sun 49
Nakba and Memories 53
Ramadan Memories 61
Moonlight 65
Thinking of spring in Palestine 67
MishMish (Apricots) & Palestine 69
Eid al-Fitr 73
Oh, Little Town of Bethlehem 79
Picnic at al Aqsa 83
Letter to Elie Wiesel 85
Abu Ali 89
Of Passover, Exile, and Deliverance 93
Sabr (cactus) Plants 97
The Victim to Guarantee His Oppressor's Security 99
Up A Tree 103
Allah works in mysterious ways 107
"Yes, yes, you call it Palestine, I call it Israel." 111
Letter to Hillary Clinton 115

This, Too, I Will Remember 121
Kindness 123
Mint Tea 125
Aunt Jamila (Um Ali) 127
The Legend of "Jaber Yassein" 131
Covering Up Crimes 135
Unexpected Privilage 137
Baby Blue Cadillac 139
A Haunting Memory 143
Teaching Hatred 145
At Gunpoint 149
Life is Beautiful 151
A Sign of Respect 155
Seedless Fruit 157
Friendship and Trust 159

Dedication

To my beloved mother (AY), who taught me how to live, and to the brave children of Gaza, who continue my education.

Memories

If one had to choose one day in their childhood that is forever ingrained in their memory as pure nirvana, mine is "that one day in spring, running through my family's orchard, trees in full blossom of pink, white, and yellow hues, birds singing, bees buzzing, blossoms floating gently in the breeze, and me? Running and dodging the trees and their branches...running with the scented wind in my face for *no* reason whatsoever, without care...just pure, unadulterated *joy* of childhood."

A memory I will cherish till my last breath!

First Love

I cannot say for sure when it happened. Nor can I say how it happened, but rest assured it happened. I had fallen hard for this, my first love. I was smitten but could not explain how or why. I was a child who could not describe my feelings for this fair maiden, the true extent of which did not reveal themselves until much later and only after I was separated from her. The vast distance between us only made me yearn more for her. She was in my blood, and there was nothing on this earth that could remove her.

Her name is Palestine. I first laid eyes on her on December 1st, 1960, the day I was born onto her soil and drew my first life-giving breath from her sacred air. She nourished me with food grown in her earth, watered by her dew, and this mixed with and formed my flesh and blood.

It was not until 1965 that I saw and felt her beauty and warmth. I was an inquisitive and adventurous child raised in the village of Beit Hanina, a suburb of Jerusalem.

I spent days upon days exploring the hills and trees that encircled the village of my youth, running from my family's fruit and olive orchards to the caves in the hills. I was never at a loss for adventure. A slingshot, handmade from olive wood, and the rubber of a car inner tube were my constant companions. All the children in the village had slingshots dangling from their back pockets: one's proficiency and marksmanship with a slingshot was a source of pride amongst the youth.

How can I describe a love affair between a man and his land? The early spring mornings with richly colored hills alive with wildflowers, plants, and blossoming trees watered by life-giving spring rains.

Standing on the high balcony my great-grandfather built, overlooking the valleys and distant hills, I saw what he had seen, admired, and loved: an ancient grape vine planted in the early 1900s, snaking its way up the staircase, covering the balcony, providing shelter and protection from the hot summer sun, its lush emerald canopy's leaves rolled by my mother, grandmother, and sisters with tender, loving hands into a staple of our daily food, as were the giant bunches of golden grapes, hanging just above my head, dangling in the breeze.

I would climb the hills where my other grandfather lived and scan the valley below, seeing my village and the mosque's minaret — my compass from every point.

To the west was my family's fruit orchards, a living carpet of green, pink, and white blossoms. The' fields, hills, and valleys were alive, with village people tending their crops and orchards. Mule and horse-drawn plows tilled the orchards and open fields, turning over long, straight lines of fresh earth as the plows dug up the dirt. Shepherds and their herds of sheep and goats, baby lambs born in the early spring months, dotted the hills, grazing on new grasses, plants, and flowers.

To the east, my family's fig and olive orchards and fields of red poppies waved in the breeze. The women of the village roamed the hills, collecting various herbs and plants to season our daily food and heal our wounds and illnesses. Whatever was not used immediately was dried and saved for later.

My mother assigned me to guard duty at the edge of one of our groves where the plums and apricots were grown. My job was to keep the girls from the neighboring girls' school away from the trees and their fruit. The girls loved to pick the small, unripe, and still green fruits—these are sour, and the girls dipped them in salt and munched them for snacks, likewise, the green almonds, so abundant in Palestine.

My mother, bless her, used to make pickles from about anything: green plums, apricots, and almonds, as well as the usual cucumbers, eggplant, and green tomatoes. All our vegetables were grown in our gardens.

Summer, with its heat, helped ripen the golden apricots, plums of every color of the rainbow, fuzzy peaches, and other fruits that were in abundance. The early summer months meant the apricot harvest, later the plums and peaches, and finally, grapes and figs that ripen only in late summer.

Nothing has stuck in my mind more than the early mornings, waking at dawn and running down to our orchards to collect fallen apricots from the ground, the ones ripened by Mother Nature and still covered by the cool, early morning dew that waters the Palestinian countryside in the summer months in the absence of rains.

I would select one of these golden beauties, lift it above my gaping mouth, and squeeze the drops of golden sweet nectar onto my tongue. The taste still lingers with me today, thirty-five years later, never duplicated.

My mother transformed what we did not consume into jams and jellies – so that year-round, we enjoyed our land's abundant and delicious fruits.

Fall ushered in the olive harvest, the most celebrated of harvests in Palestine. Olive trees can live for many hundreds of years and are a very vital part of Palestinian life. Cared for as one would for a newborn child, olive trees are synonymous with Palestine and her people. The orchards and their crops are an integral part of Palestinian life.

The olive harvests were festivals when the hills and valleys become alive with people; entire families and scores of people carry ladders and sacks as they make their way to harvest their precious crops. The olive harvest was, by far, my favorite season of the year. I loved to be with my siblings as we picked olives and ate our meals under the trees my ancestors had planted and harvested before me, where they ate, like me, under the same trees hundreds of years before.

After the harvest, olives are either turned, cracked, pickled, or sent to the nearby presses to become the best cold-pressed virgin olive oil on the planet. To this day, I still receive olive oil from my mother pressed from the olives grown on our lands: the same trees my ancestors harvested and I climbed and harvested as a youth.

We spent the winter months quietly indoors. There was no electricity in the village then. We burned wood to heat our humble abode. A large metal barrel, with both ends cut off, would be placed atop the round stove; the wood piled into the barrel, and the fire lit. After the wood had become glowing embers, it would be carried inside to heat the house. Some used kerosene heaters, but most used these simple wood-burning stoves that I loved.

As kids, we would take eggs and bury them in the hot ashes of the fire to roast. After a few moments, they were ready to be taken out and eaten. The taste was so much better than simple boiled eggs. Sometimes, we would bury potatoes and other vegetables to get them cooked. The elders would make coffee and tea at the edge of the glowing embers.

The winter months brought the much-needed rains, even the occasional snowfall. The kids loved the snowfalls. We would run outside to play in the snow, knowing full well it would melt fast when it touched the earth.

The snow-covered hills were a rare and awesome sight, and the olive trees covered in snow were also a remarkable sight.

Families huddled by the fire, exchanging stories and tales handed down for generations. We also had an old radio, but we usually provided our own entertainment, giving root to an indescribable feeling of closeness with community and family. Such life made me fall madly in love with my beautiful Palestine. Her soil intermixed with my blood, her air fills my lungs, and her beauty is forever displayed in the museum of my mind. One never forgets his first love...

Today, my village is barely recognizable from what I remember. It is encircled now by Jewish settlements that seem to dominate and choke her. There is a Jewish-only highway that cuts straight through the heart of my beloved Beit Hanina like a giant scar on an otherwise beautiful face.

Most of the olive orchards have been destroyed and uprooted by the Israelis in their unquenchable thirst for land. The village is cut in half; its people are not allowed to travel from one side to the other – not even when their lands are there. The residents are cut off from their lands, crops, orchards, and, more importantly, families by roadblocks and soldiers.

Palestine today is a land bleeding and in pain. May the grace of God heal the wounds and mend their broken hearts so that she may know true peace.

If I close my eyes and think hard enough, I can still see what made me fall madly in love with my homeland. Yes, she has changed. And yes, she has a few scars, some wrinkles, and lines, but these only make me more attracted to her – my first and true love.

Today's Dinner

I write this considering the recent Israeli claims (cultural theft) on yet another Palestinian dish and as a tribute to my late father-in-law (ay).

My wife made a large pot of stuffed grape leaves for the family dinner today. She had spent most of the day carefully rolling the grape leaves into finger-sized morsels. God bless her hands and talents, for she is one fantastic cook, *almost* as good as my mother, and that is saying quite a bit!

Why am I writing about grape leaves currently? Well, let me explain and give some background to the grape leaves we had for dinner today.

In 1969, two years after Israel invaded and conquered the West Bank, Palestinians were finally permitted to visit parts of Palestine that became Israel after 1948. One of those places was my father-in-law's home village of Lifta. In 1948, the Zionists attacked and conquered Lifta, forcing the residents to flee, and the ones who stayed behind were taken by truck and dumped into east Jerusalem, which was still in Arab hands.

The Palestinian residents of Lifta left most of their possessions, homes, trees, and orchards behind as they instantly became homeless refugees. The Palestinian homes that remained had holes blown into their roofs and floors by the Zionists to ensure the villagers would not return because their homes were now made "uninhabitable."

In the summer of 1969, my father-in-law ventured back to the village of his birth. It had been twenty long years since he had last set foot in his ancestral village. After walking around a bit, he came upon a large grapevine. With no one to take care of this vine, it had grown "wild" all over the courtyard of an abandoned house. After getting a closer look, he noticed large bunches of grapes were dangling from the vine. He ate a few of the golden grapes, their taste awakening his senses and bringing forth an avalanche of memories. He then decided to take a couple with him to his house in the Ramallah area refugee camp!

Once back home in his humble abode, he gave his daughters a "taste of home" by allowing them to each try the grapes of Lifta. As he and his family ate the grapes, they threw the seeds into the flower beds he had built in front of his house. A few weeks later, a grapevine sprouted from the ground. One of the seeds had taken root and was now growing into a grapevine, transplanted as it were, away from its home and surroundings, much like the people of the village of Lifta.

And so, the grapevine grew and grew, with my father-in-law tending to it as if it were a small child, watering and pruning it. It became his obsession, a passion. As it grew, he erected metal bars and wires overhead, covering the entire front area of the house and the tiny little "courtyard" of his hovel in the dust-choked refugee camp of Al-Khadura.

The grapevine, much like a grateful "child," rewarded the old man's love and devotion, producing year after year an abundance of grapes, "golden drops of honey," as he liked to refer to them. The grapevine, which eventually grew to cover the entire area surrounding the house, spilling over to the neighbor's home, produced such an abundance of grapes he distributed to his many neighbors in the overcrowded camp.

Also, apart from the tasty grapes, the grapevine's tender young leaves proved ideal for rolling and stuffing some of the best-tasting grape leaves around because they had a naturally "tangy" flavor.

Eventually, there were more tender grape leaves than his family could consume in a growing season, so they started to pack them away for use in winter when fresh leaves were no longer available.

As in many rural parts of Palestine, up to the 1970s, there was no electricity and no refrigerators or freezers to freeze vegetables and other staples for later use. Many Palestinians would "can" many vegetables, including grape leaves. My mother-in-law thought that "pickling" the grape leaves took away from their flavor. She preferred to pick them fresh, roll them tight, and insert them through the small opening of plastic bottles, fill up the bottle as much as possible, then place the cap on tightly. She put them away for later use —a crude and early form of vacuum packing. This proved an ideal way to store the grape leaves, locking in the flavor and freshness.

This brings me back to the tasty stuffed grape leaves dinner my talented wife made for us today.

Last year, while we were in Palestine for the summer, my eighty-eight-year-old father-in-law would climb on a ladder each morning, reaching high to the new growths, and pick a couple of handfuls of grape leaves and hand them to my mother-in-law. Seeing him teetering up on a ladder like that caused his daughters much worry, but he insisted on doing this himself and would not allow anyone else to pick the leaves, claiming they did not know the "prime leaves from grass."

One morning, I asked him why he was doing this, and he replied that he wanted his grandchildren (my kids) to have the best grape leaves to eat when they returned to America.

Just before we left Ramallah for the last time, after many teary farewells, the most heart-wrenching moment was when he hugged my youngest son, Omar, holding him tight, and said, "I hope that when you come to visit me again next year, I will be here for you."

My sister-in-law handed me four 1-liter plastic soda bottles filled with the grape leaves that my father-in-law had been picking each morning.

So, you see, the grape leaves that we ate today have a history and a story behind them, much like the refugees of Palestine. They did not just appear from thin air, nor were they "manufactured" …From a seed!

When we returned to Palestine in the summer of 2005, my father-in-law would no longer be able to pick fresh grape leaves for us to take back to America. About a month ago, doctors amputated his leg, at first below the knee, then the rest of it. The main reason for the amputation was the lack of access to medical treatment due to Israel's oppressive and inhumane roadblocks and checkpoints.

So, as we sat down to eat our dinner today, I noticed that my wife's eyes were welling up with tears as she asked God to "bless the hands that picked these."

Below are pictures of my late father-in-law's grape vines. He passed away in 2015, still longing to return to the home and village that the Zionists forced him to leave.

The home in Ramallah's Kadoura Refugee Camp has since been torn down, and with it, the grapevines.

Desecrating the memory of Babe Ruth

When former NY City Mayor Giuliani contemplated running for President, he likened Ariel Sharon to Baseball legend Babe Ruth, which, as a *huge* baseball fan, moved me to write the following Essay published in 2005...

I was appalled to read that, while on a speaking tour in Israel, Former New York City Mayor Rudolph Giuliani said Sharon reminds him of baseball legend Babe Ruth. How Mr. Giuliani arrived at the conclusion of comparing Ariel, "the butcher of Beirut," Sharon and Babe, and "the sultan of swat" Ruth is beyond even my wildest imagination.

I was born In Palestine and came to America at the age of eight in 1969; soon afterward, I discovered baseball and grew to love the game with all its subtle nuances, idiosyncrasies, and rich and wonderful history.

As a youngster, I learned how to play baseball in the youth league named after baseball legend Babe Ruth (the Babe Ruth League). It did not take long to fall in love with the game, and as I became better at it, the more I wanted to learn about its history, reading as many books as I could find in our small school library about the sport and the many colorful and gifted players who played it.

In fifth Grade, we were assigned to write a report on our favorite athlete or personality. Although I was a huge Detroit Tigers fan, I skipped past legends Ty Cobb, Al Kaline, and Mickey Cochrane and decided to do my report on George Herman Ruth Jr., "the Babe," and The Great "Bambino."

I checked out a few books about Babe Ruth and the great New York Yankee teams of the 20s and 30s, when the Yankees dominated baseball, especially the 1929 team, which is still widely regarded as the greatest baseball team of all time.

For more than twenty years, Babe Ruth was the most famous athlete in America as he tore through the record books with his superhuman exploits on the field. Children were naturally attracted to the larger-than-life Babe, and he to them, spending much of his time in their company.

By the time he retired in 1935, Babe Ruth, through his feats on the baseball diamond and lifestyle, had achieved legendary status in New York and the entire country. In 1936, he was among the first five baseball players to be inducted into the Baseball Hall of Fame.

Babe Ruth's popularity and fame were so widespread that even America's enemies knew of him. A decade after he had bashed his last home run, his presence still was felt.

His record of sixty homers in 1927 stood up for thirty-four years.

During World War II, when Japanese soldiers charged American troops, they would sometimes scream, "To hell with Babe Ruth." Not "to hell with FDR" or "to hell with Douglas MacArthur," but "to hell with Babe Ruth."

What bigger compliment could an American receive?

Ruth was a man of mythic proportions. He became even more than the ultimate American sports celebrity. He was "a unique figure in the social history of the United States," wrote Robert Creamer in *Babe: The Legend Comes to Life*. "For more than any other man, Babe Ruth transcended sports, moved far beyond the artificial limits of baselines and outfield fences and sports pages."

After writing my report and presenting it to the whole class in a Yankee Jersey with the number "3" stitched on the back, signifying the number Babe Ruth wore on his Yankee uniform, I was instantly transformed into a fan of the Great Bambino. This fascination is still with me today.

How Rudy Giuliani could ever compare the war criminal Ariel Sharon, a man whose hands are soaked with the blood of thousands of innocent men, women, and children to the loveable, smiling Yankee giant is sacrilegious.

The only thing that Babe Ruth ever destroyed was baseballs and records, unlike Ariel Sharon, who was also known as the "bulldozer" for his penchant for wreaking havoc and destruction on the Palestinian people, their property, and their rights.

There are many photographs of Babe Ruth smiling, playing, and signing autographs while surrounded by large groups of smiling children. On the other hand, there are many gruesome photographs of dead and horrified Palestinian children in the wake of a "visit" by Ariel Sharon.

Babe Ruth used to stop in the middle of residential neighborhoods and throw the ball to small children as he played catch with them, while Ariel Sharon and his infamous and brutal Unit 101 were documented throwing hand grenades through the windows of Palestinian homes where children were cowering in fear with their parents.

Looking at the 1930's era watch with the smiling Great Babe Ruth on the dial prominently displayed on my office desk, I know of no two human beings who could be more different from each other than the Babe and Israeli Prime Minister Ariel Sharon.

In the world of "political prostitution," whereby Rudy Giuliani hopes that by cuddling up to Ariel Sharon and his Zionist constituency, they will help him in his eventual bid to become the next president of the United States, desecrating the name and memory of an American icon by comparing him to a war criminal is "acceptable," but not to this longtime fan of the Babe and the concept of justice.

Alfi laila wa laila

One day, while listening to Oum Kulthoum (by myself since my kids don't appreciate her as much as I do, although they love Arabic music in general, they think she is "boring") and tending to my little trees, my mind drifted to the first time I had ever heard the legendary Oum Kulthoum, the single greatest singer in the Arab world, whose popularity was and still is unmatched, even after she had died more than thirty years ago!

Her songs, especially the patriotic and moving songs I had heard as a child during the 1967 war and after, stirred in me emotions I had never felt before. Grown men would have tears welling up in their eyes and lumps in their throats at the sound of her voice!

When it was announced that the Egyptian radio station would be broadcasting her concert, in which she sang "Alfi laila wa laila" (thousand and one night) in the spring of 1969 (I was eight and getting ready to immigrate to America with my mother), I remember the streets being empty in our village as all of the men ran home or congregated in coffeehouses to listen to her sing.

I took our old battery-operated radio (we had no electricity) and sat in my favorite place, the huge windowsill of our home, overlooking the courtyard, where my mother planted a dizzying array of fragrant flowers, spices, and vegetables. I especially loved the soothing, delicate scent of the jasmine plant that climbed the side of the house and right next to my window. When the cool breeze blew, it would fill the house with the pleasant aroma of the jasmine blossoms.

After hearing that song, almost an entire hour in length, I instantly became a fan of Oum Kulthoum, singing the song over and over to myself as I ran and played in the hills and orchards of my village, forever linking the song, the cool breeze, and the heavenly scent of my mother's jasmine plant. At that exact point in time, I was as close to "heaven" as humanly possible for an eight-year-old child.

Towards the end of summer in 1969, much to my anger and dismay, my mother and I immigrated to the US to join my father and the rest of my brothers and sisters who had gone there earlier.

Upon arriving in Detroit, Michigan, I was no longer exposed to Arabic music, let alone Oum Kulthoum, hearing it only when I rode in my father's car. Most of the time, I had to listen to Motown Music, which was the rage then, especially in the predominantly African American neighborhood where my dad owned a small grocery store.

After many months of listening to that type of music, I soon stopped humming the Arabic songs of Oum Kulthoum in my head. I was now trying to sing along with the Supremes, Stevie Wonder, Smoky Robinson, Marvin Gaye, and the host of popular singers that Detroit was producing.

Later, when my dad sold his store and bought another one, this time in a predominantly white ethnic neighborhood in Detroit, I started to listen to more Rock and Roll, again, forgetting all about the music I had loved as a child in Palestine.

The stereo in the store played Rock and Roll, day and night, and I was now singing along to the Beatles, Rolling Stones, Jimmy Hendrix, Led Zeppelin, Aero Smith, and the rest of the popular rock bands of the 1970s. This lasted through my high school years until the summer of 1979 — Oum Kulthoum died in 1975. Four million people were on the streets of Cairo for her funeral. Grown men, like my father, cried at the news of her death. Although I saw the large funeral in the streets of Cairo on TV, I did not really "feel" anything then.

In the summer of 1979, right after I graduated from high school, I made my first trip back to Palestine since I had left in the summer of 1969. My mother returned to Palestine in the spring of 1971, electing to give birth to my brother in Palestine rather than in America.

Upon arrival, I noticed that many things had changed, some for the better but quite a bit more for the worse. Our village was finally connected to the Jerusalem electric grid and now had electricity. Television antennas, non-existent as I was growing up, were now on every roof top. Also, the Israeli policy of building settlements on lands confiscated from their Palestinian owners was now in full swing after the Israeli/Egyptian Accords at Camp David. In Beit Hanina, the Jewish settlement of Neve Yacouve was being built, and the large settlement of Ramot Allon, which loomed menacingly above Beit Hanina, was built on the village's hills to the south.

I awoke early the first morning "back home" and walked around our home, inspecting every tree, plant, and flower in my mother's overcrowded courtyard garden. Much to my pleasure, the things I had remembered fondly as a child were still there, including the magnificent jasmine plant, which was more like a tree now as it snaked its way up and around the window to the roof of our ancient home.

After breakfast, I went to the center of the village. Then I made my way to our orchards, which were filled with apricots, plums, and other fruit trees, and then finally, to my favorite part, the hills that dominated our landscape, where, as a child, I had spent countless hours playing, flying kites, and exploring.

After a few hours in the hot summer sun, I decided to head back to our house, get a cold drink, and cool off. My mother greeted me with a pitcher of homemade lemonade, made from the freshly squeezed lemons that grew on the tree in her garden and fresh mint leaves for added flavor.

I poured a large glass and made my way to the windowsill, which now did not seem as large as I remembered. I sat before the open window, relishing the cool jasmine-scented breeze wafting through it, and plugged in the new radio I had brought as a gift for my little brother. I fumbled with the dial, trying to find Arabic radio stations amid the many Hebrew and English stations that were not around when I was a kid.

After a few moments, I finally dialed in a radio station from Cairo, Egypt. Soon after a song by Abdel Halim Hafez had finished, the unmistakable beginning of Oum Kulthoum's song, "*Alfi laila wa laila*," emanated from the radio. Goosebumps and a shiver ran through my body. I was, for an instant, transposed to a place ten years earlier in my life.

Memories suppressed for ten years bubbled near the surface for that whole time and were now gushing forth like a tidal wave.

I sat there for two hours, reflecting, thinking, and most of all, remembering… Remembering my childhood, the war, my village, our trips to Jerusalem, remembering Palestine!

Like the olive trees in my home in America when I planted them in front of the window, facing east, I too experienced a "new growth and appreciation" of my homeland, of its earth, rocks, trees, and the scent of delicate jasmine blossoms, carried by the cool afternoon breeze through an ancient hand-built home in Palestine, while the Great Lady from Egypt sang, "a thousand and one night."

The Olive Harvest

Olive trees have always held a special place in my heart and memories. The olive tree and the groves are an integral part of the very fabric of Palestinian life. This is the reason that Jewish terrorists target Palestinian olive trees, burning, chopping, and uprooting them to inflict pain on the population.

I wish to share my memories of the olive harvests I experienced as a young boy in Palestine.

I always anticipated the annual olive harvest with great joy, much more so than the time to harvest the many fruits grown on my family's land. We carefully inspected each tree throughout the year to ensure a healthy harvest.

My mother followed a practice of tying a piece of black linen to a branch of those trees that promised an exceptionally abundant crop — this helped ward off the "evil eyes" that might have a negative effect on the tree and its harvest. [This is a custom much like a mother placing a blue stone or a silver hand with an eye on a carriage or affixed to a baby's chest, an amulet to protect the child and ward off evil spirits.] The black cloth (or the blue stone) would distract a person from looking at the promising olive crop with envy. Superstition was evident when it came to protecting the olive trees, just as it reflects how much importance and love there was for the olive trees.

When the olive harvesting season begins, the hillsides become alive with families working to gather their precious crops. To this day, family members travel to one another's fields from all over the country to help in the olive harvest.

Olives are picked by hand as they have been for thousands of years. As a child, I joined my family as we set out early in the day with a picnic of cracked olives, tomatoes, cheese, sardines, onions, freshly baked bread, and, of course, the ever-present thermos of mint tea. We took the food bundled the night before and carried large blankets, heavy ladders, and burlap bags as we headed for the hills with the olive groves.

Once there, we spread the blankets under the tree, and the ladders leaned against it. My mother and sisters picked olives they could by hand and used sticks or shook branches to knock down the ones too high to reach.

As for me, I loved to climb, and climb I did. I would bounce from one branch to another, giving my mother a heart attack in the process. I played around a lot more than I picked olives in those days. I loved being outdoors with my family. I would get to the top of these beautiful and ancient trees and proceed to throw olives at my sisters and brothers below me, an act that usually elicited no end to threats of bodily harm from my siblings. My mother spent more time yelling at me than anything else.

My grandfather (God bless his soul) often yelled at his daughter, my mother, "Stop yelling at the boy, let him have fun."

We were Fellaheen (farmers), and as a fellah child, I lived for the outdoors. This was the place where I was the happiest. We had no electricity and, thus, no TV to distract me. The hills, trees, and orchards were my playground.

My grandfather often entertained me with stories from his youth about the trees and the harvest.

Widowed at forty, he never remarried and lived to the ripe old age of ninety-eight. He was a vegetarian long before it became fashionable. He lived on Zaatar (wild thyme that grew in the hills), olives, tomatoes, and fresh bread. He walked upright and smoked his pipe right up to the day he died in 1978. Grandpa used to walk five to ten kilometers a day. He was always walking somewhere. He was the only one of my grandparents who was still alive when I was born. The last time I saw him was in 1969.

Anyhow, after we gathered the olives, we placed them in large bags and carried them back home to be spread on the roof of our house for a few days before being sent to the village presses at Bir Zeit (in Arabic, an oil well). Not all olives were sent to the presses; my mom made some into the pickled cracked olives that are so famous in Palestine.

We used medium-sized stones like hammers to crack the olives one by one. Other olives were left to ripen in the sun and then stored with salt and oil. Olives thus prepared are still seen in the many markets of Palestine. They are usually black and look like mini prunes.

The olive trees and the land they grow on still have a special place in my heart. They offer me a sense of connection to my history and my people. A sense that is reinforced each time I remember or climb a tree planted several hundred years before by my ancestors. Thinking that I was picking and eating from the same trees my people had picked and eaten olives from for generations before me inspires awe. I will most assuredly pass on it to my children, and I hope they will get the chance to do likewise.

Thus, I offer you the following:

The Olive tree...

God created it before man

A branch in the bill of a dove that heralded peace and security for Noah...

Palestinians care for newly planted trees as if they were newborn children

When the Palestinians plant an olive tree, they say a prayer. "God protect it and make it grow so that my children's grandchildren will benefit from its abundance."

What are the Israelis saying by uprooting and destroying the ancient orchards of olive trees?

Love and Refugees

All Successive Israeli governments and Zionist-based policies have had one single goal in common: To wage wars on the Palestinian refugees.

These wars seek to finish the job the Zionists started after 1948. The Israeli army had attacked and ravaged these poor and destitute remnants of Palestine. The Zionists have been and continue wishing that the refugees would just "go away" (and so it seems the rest of the World). They have done and are continually doing everything possible to achieve this end, whether by brute force, coercion, or sheer propaganda!

First, there was the denial that an actual Palestinian people ever existed. When this warped and twisted line failed, they then denied that the creation of the State of Israel was the root cause of the refugee problem. The Zionists blamed the Arab world for causing the Palestinians to flee their homes. They made no mention of the ethnic cleansing or brutality that was the basis of the Zionists' attitude toward the original inhabitants of the land.

In the early 1900s, an exploratory delegation of Rabbis was sent to Palestine to assess and report back to the World Zionists Organization. They reported back with a "coded phrase" to their European brethren with this famous statement: "The Bride is beautiful, but she is married to another man."

The "bride" was Palestine, and the husband was the multitude of Palestinians that were living there. The Zionists knew full well that to steal the bride, they had to get rid of the husband.

They embarked on a widespread campaign to convince the world that Palestine was "a fair maiden" who needed a husband. That this "fair maiden" could only realize her full potential and prosper if and only if the right husband were found for her. They argued that God had promised her hand to a Jewish husband. Only by marrying a Jew could she be "redeemed."

Secondly, using terror, murder, lies, and deception, they forced the Palestinians to flee their land. They thought that the Palestinians would just move to other Arab countries and forget about their ancestral homes. They did not realize the strength of the Palestinian's attachment to their land. The husband was still very much in love with his "wife." The Palestinians would not give up on their land.

The Zionist policy then shifted to inflicting pain and suffering on all Palestinian refugees as an ongoing policy. These criminals reasoned that if the Israeli army kept up a war on the Palestinian refugees, they would succumb, thus driving them to despair and finally to give up any hope of returning to their land. We have seen this in the successive wars that Sharon and his band of criminals have waged, from the early massacres of the small villages in the late 40s, to the 50s and 60s in Gaza and the West Bank refugee camps to the 70s and 80s in Lebanon (Sabra and Shatila being just a few), to the present day attacks on the refugee camps in Gaza and the West Bank.

Make no mistake. The true war is on the collective will and conscience of the Palestinian people in general and the refugees in particular. The Zionists' goal is to cause despair, hopelessness, and finally surrender amongst the refugees. These goals have failed miserably and will never be achieved. The Palestinians have never been more determined. Justice is what they seek. No amount of terror will weaken their will.

For you see, the husband has never abandoned his first love. He has and always will love his "bride" and seek to be reunited with her...

"The Israeli Experience"

A few years back, I believe it was the summer of 2006, when I waited for six *long* for a relative to arrive at Ben Gurion Airport, I had a chance to see more than 300 young Jews from around the globe arrive as part of "The Israeli Experience" program whereby they bring high school-aged youngsters and let them "experience" Israel…

In the airport's arrival promenade, huge concrete columns supporting the reception area were decorated with balloons and confetti, and each had a number on it.

Before the teenagers came through the doors, they were assigned to a group, heading to their designated areas, where each was greeted by young, good-looking Israeli soldiers in uniform (no guns). A male soldier greeted the female students and the males by a perky female soldier in a tight-fitting uniform.

One by one, the soldiers hugged these gangly teenagers (it looked very awkward, and some seemed to be not so "comfortable" by this public show, but after the hugs, the female soldier would lock arms with a male "guest" and do a little dance (the same for the male soldier and female guest) reminiscent of an old fashioned "country style hoe-down" as the others clapped and sang in English, "This is how we party! This is how we party! Israel loves to party!"

They did this for each of their young "guests" …

Israeli soldiers (only the "good looking ones") serve as camp "counselors" and chaperones for these young Jews as they "experience Israel" in the constant company of these IDF "ambassadors."

The picture of what the Zionist government is trying to accomplish is crystal clear. They want to plant the "seeds" for future

IDF service in the fertile, confused minds of these teenagers, and they do so by making it seem "fun."

In the Zionist State, there exists a widespread culture of hate and racism. The actions of the IDF in Gaza and elsewhere are *not* "isolated" cases as they would have the world believe, but a prevalent and systematic approach to the Palestinian Arabs, their lives, rights, and property.

One time, while waiting at the "Hizma" checkpoint, I noticed a young Israeli soldier putting Palestinian men, women, and children in the crosshairs of his gun. He pretended to "shoot" them one by one (he was providing the soundtrack as he pretended to pull the trigger), and his friends were laughing.

He was an American serving his summer in the service of the IDF and was bored and "itching" for some action, as his friends explained to me.

Truly a disturbing sight, but made all that much more bizarre was the fact that he sang Britney Spears' song "Crazy" as he pretended to blow off the heads of Palestinians while they waited in long lines to cross the checkpoint.

Does one's "Birthright" enable and encourage oppression, brutality, and crimes against humanity?

Apparently, in Israel, it does, and so much more!

Benny Morris and Ethnic Cleansing

I read Benny Morris's op-ed piece in the LA Times last week, in which he stated, "In '48 Israel Did What It Had to Do."

I have since spent many hours pondering his conclusion. His justification for the ethnic cleansing, rape, and murder of the Palestinian people to facilitate the founding of the Jewish state left me numb. Ethnic cleansing, rape, and murder were justified as a means to an end.

Although I was born in Palestine and moved to the US at the age of eight, I was, like most Americans, bombarded by the Zionist accounts of the "brave and moral" Zionist underdogs fighting for survival against the "backward, bloodthirsty savages." There was never any mention of the crimes and atrocities visited upon the Palestinian inhabitants. The stories and narratives of the Zionists I read and seen had a kind of "rugged romanticism" to them that smacked of a typical Hollywood Western. The Zionists were the "cowboys," and the Palestinians were cast in the role of the "Indians."

The Palestinian narrative and history were suppressed and, in most cases, denied to the outside world. If one wanted to find anything about Israel, there was ample propaganda-filled material, which never missed the chance to further the image of the Zionists and malign the "Arabs" for the word "Palestinians" did not exist as far as they were concerned.

Being a Palestinian, I, of course, knew much of what had happened to my people at the hands of the Zionist founders of the state of Israel. I had heard many first-hand accounts from my family members.

My grandmother's village of Lifta, located in the Jerusalem District, was ethnically cleansed of its inhabitants. Members of the Jewish terrorist gang, probably from Begin's IZL or the Stern gang, had attacked the village on December 28th, 1947. The terrorists jumped out of a bus and mowed down the men who sat in the village coffeehouse. Nine men were killed, and many were injured. My father-in-law was amongst the survivors of this vicious attack. He escaped death by lying still and pretending he was dead.

Lifta was mostly destroyed except for a few deserted houses (including the village mosque and its club) and some houses homeless and hippie Israelis used. Soon after the terror act on Lifta's coffee house, its population was terrorized repeatedly into leaving by Menachem Begin's IZL and Yitzhak Shamir's Stern terror gangs. By February 1948, the village was completely emptied, and all its inhabitants were trucked to East Jerusalem.

Fifty-five years after he and his fellow villagers were ethnically cleansed from their homes, my father-in-law, who is eighty-seven, still lives in a refugee camp, having been denied the right to return to his home and property. Fifty-five years later, my father-in-law sat with his grandchildren (including my children, who were born and raised in the US) and recounted his vivid memories and details that led to his life as a refugee. I wonder if Mr. Morris and his fellow advocates of war crimes such as ethnic cleansing would be willing to sit, look them in the face, and explain to my children, whom I have raised to be respectful and tolerant of all human beings, in the presence of their grandfather, that the Zionists founders were "only doing what had to be done," and that the circumstances of their grandparents' suffering were just a means to an end: the creation of a "Jewish" state.

To this day, the relentless quest to ethnically cleanse Palestinians from the land between the River Jordan and the Sea is still going on. Only now, it is less "noticeable" to the outside world. Israeli leaders openly talk of the term "transfer," a coded word for ethnic cleansing.

In a world where barriers have come tumbling down, Israel is erecting them to imprison and torture the Palestinian people.

I remember that in 6th grade, we were made to watch a movie called "Man's Inhumanity to Man." This was my first real exposure to the atrocities perpetrated against the Jews by the Nazis. The horrific pictures of the piles of corpses, shot in grainy black and white, were a shock to me. I was both saddened and angry at the treatment of humans at the hands of other humans.

Later that year, I read The Diary of Anne Frank. It gave me further insight into the Jewish suffering and trauma. Then I watched the Holocaust mini-series Schindler's List, and one of my all-time favorites, Life is Beautiful. While watching all these movies and the accounts of Jewish suffering, I could not help but wonder why these same people who have suffered so much for so long had, in turn, inflicted and continued to inflict much suffering on my people. I identified with Anne Frank and her experiences. I have made it a point that every one of my children also reads Anne Frank.

How sad would it be to try to explain to my children, using Mr. Morris's logic, that the Nazis were "only doing what had to be done" to have a "racially pure" nation?

"Thanking" Sharon

Since the so-called Gaza disengagement, US President George W Bush has reiterated his call that people ought to be "thanking Ariel Sharon" for keeping Israel's word about dismantling its occupation of Palestinian territory.

What does Sharon's history tell us?

Sharon's first documented sortie in the role George W Bush describes as a "man of peace" was in August of 1953 in the refugee camp of El-Bureig, south of Gaza. An Israeli history of "Unit 101" records fifty refugees as having been killed; other sources allege fifteen or twenty.

Major-General Vagn Bennike, the UN commander, reported that "bombs were thrown" by Sharon's men "through the windows of huts in which the refugees were sleeping and, as they fled, they were attacked by small arms and automatic weapons."

In October of 1953 came the attack by Sharon's Unit 101 on the Jordanian village of Qibya, whose "stain" Israel's foreign minister at the time, Moshe Sharett (aka Shertok), confided to his diary "would stick to us and not be washed away for many years."

He was wrong.

Pro-Israel commentators in the West compared it to Lidice, Qibya, and Sharon's role are scarcely evoked in the West today, least of all by journalists such as Deborah Sontag of the New York Times who wrote a whitewash of Sharon, describing him as "feisty," or the Washington Post's man in Jerusalem who fondly invoked him after his fateful excursion to the Holy Places in Jerusalem as "the portly old warrior."

Israeli historian Avi Shlaim describes the massacre thus: "Sharon's order was to penetrate Qibya, blow up houses, and inflict heavy casualties on its inhabitants. His success in carrying out the order surpassed all expectations. The full and macabre story of what happened at Qibya was revealed only during the morning after the attack."

The village had been reduced to rubble: forty-five houses had been blown up, and sixty-nine civilians, two-thirds of them women and children, had been killed. Sharon and his men claimed they "believed that all the inhabitants had run away and that they had no idea that anyone was hiding inside the houses."

The UN observer on the scene reached a different conclusion, "One story was repeated time after time: the bullet splintered door, the body sprawled across the threshold, indicating that the inhabitants had been forced by heavy fire to stay inside until their homes were blown up over them."

The slaughter in Qibya was described contemporaneously in a letter to the president of the United Nations Security Council dated 16 October 1953 (S/3113) from the Envoy Extraordinary and Minister Plenipotentiary of Jordan to the United States. On 14 October 1953, at 9:30 pm, he wrote, "Israeli troops launched a battalion-scale attack on the village of Qibya in the Hashemite Kingdom of Jordan (at the time the West Bank was annexed to Jordan).

According to the diplomat's account, Israeli forces had entered the village and systematically murdered all occupants of houses, using automatic weapons, grenades, and incendiaries. On 14 October, the bodies of 42 Arab civilians had been recovered; several more bodies were still under the wreckage. Forty houses, the village school, and a reservoir had been destroyed. Quantities of unused explosives bearing Israel army markings in Hebrew had been found in the village. At about 3 a.m., to cover their withdrawal, Israeli support troops had begun shelling the neighboring villages of Budrus and Shuqba from positions in Israel."

And what about Sharon's conduct when he was head of the Southern Command of Israel's Defense Forces in the early 1970s? The Gaza "clearances" were vividly described by Phil Reeves in a piece in The London Independent on January 21, 2001.

"More than thirty years have elapsed since Ariel Sharon was the head of the Israel Defense Forces' southern command, charged with the task of 'pacifying' the recalcitrant Gaza Strip after the 1967 war. But the old men still remember it well, especially the old men on Wreckage Street. Until late 1970, Wreckage, or Had'd, Street was not a street, just one of scores of narrow, nameless alleys weaving through Gaza City's Beach Camp, a shantytown cluttered with low, two-roomed houses, built with UN aid for refugees from the 1948 war who then, as now, were waiting for the international community to settle their future. The street acquired its name after an unusually prolonged visit from Mr. Sharon's soldiers. Their orders were to bulldoze hundreds of homes to carve a wide, straight street. This would allow Israeli troops and their heavy armored vehicles to move easily through the camp, exert control, and hunt down men from the Palestinian Liberation Army.

"'They came at night and began marking the houses they wanted to demolish with red paint,' said Ibrahim Ghanim, 70, a retired laborer. 'In the morning, they came back and ordered everyone to leave. I remember all the soldiers shouting at people, Yalla, yalla, yalla, yalla! They threw everyone's belongings into the street. Then Sharon brought in bulldozers and started flattening the street. He did the whole lot in one day. And the soldiers would beat people. Can you imagine soldiers with guns beating little kids? By the time the Israeli army's work was done, hundreds of homes were destroyed, not only on Wreckage Street but throughout the camp, as Sharon plowed out a grid of wide security roads.

"Many of the refugees took shelter in schools or squeezed into the already badly over-crowded homes of relatives. Other families, usually those with a Palestinian political activist, were loaded into trucks and taken to exile in a town in the heart of the Sinai Desert, then controlled by Israel."

As Reeves reported, the devastation of Beach Camp was far from the exception. "In August 1971 alone, troops under Mr. Sharon's command destroyed some 2,000 homes in the Gaza Strip, uprooting 16,000 people (about the seating capacity of Madison Square Garden) for the second time in their lives. Hundreds of young Palestinian men were arrested and deported to Jordan and Lebanon. Six hundred relatives of suspected guerrillas were exiled to Sinai. In the second half of 1971, 104 guerrillas were assassinated. 'The policy at that time was not to arrest suspects, but to assassinate them,' said Raji Sourani, director of the Palestinian Centre for Human Rights in Gaza City."

Israeli complacency leading to their initial defeat by the Egyptians in the 1973 war was in part nurtured by the impregnability of the "Bar Lev line" constructed by Sharon on the east bank of the Suez Canal. The Egyptians pierced the line without undue difficulty.

In 1981, Sharon, then minister of defense, visited Israel's good friend, President Mobutu of Zaire. Lunching on Mobutu's yacht, the Israeli party was asked by their host to use their good offices to get the US Congress to be more forthcoming with aid. This, the Israelis managed to accomplish. As a quid pro quo, Mobutu reestablished diplomatic relations with Israel.

This was not Sharon's only contact with Africa. Among friends, he relays fond memories of trips to Angola to observe and advise the South African forces, then fighting in support of the CIA stooge Jonas Savimbi.

As defense minister in Menachem Begin's second government, Sharon was the commander who led the full-dress 1982 assault on Lebanon, with the express design of destroying the PLO, driving as many Palestinians as possible to Jordan, and making Lebanon a client state of Israel.

It was a war plan that cost untold suffering, around 20,000 Palestinian and Lebanese lives, and the deaths of over one thousand

Israeli soldiers. The Israelis bombed civilian populations at will. Sharon also oversaw the infamous massacres at Sabra and Shatila refugee camps.

The Lebanese government counted 762 bodies recovered and a further 1,200 buried privately by relatives. (Was Lebanon spared a nuclear assault? Just as the 1982 war was getting underway, Sharon approached Menachem Begin, then Prime Minister, and suggested that begin ceding control over Israel's atomic weapons trigger to him. Begin refused.)

The slaughter in the two contiguous camps at Sabra and Shatila took place from 6:00 at night on September 16, 1982, until 8:00 in the morning on September 18, 1982, in an area under the control of the Israel Defense Forces. The perpetrators were members of the Phalange militia, the Lebanese force that was armed by and closely allied with Israel since the onset of Lebanon's civil war in 1975. The victims during the 62-hour rampage included infants, children, women (including pregnant women), and the elderly, some of whom were mutilated or disemboweled before or after they were killed.

An official Israeli commission of inquiry – chaired by Yitzhak Kahan, president of Israel's Supreme Court – investigated the massacre and, in February 1983, publicly released its findings. This was published without Appendix B, which remains secret until now. Never acknowledged in Israel, despite its exposure at the time by Radio France's Beirut correspondent, is the role — inside Sabra and Shatila, alongside the Phalange gangs — of Sayerret Maskal, the Israeli army's version of the British SAS. This unit had been implicated in marking for assassination the residences of teachers, nurses, doctors, journalists, and any others suspected of having or likely to have connections beyond the camp, including access to international media.

Amid desperate attempts to cover up the evidence of direct knowledge of what was going on by Israeli military personnel, the Kahan Commission found itself compelled to find that Ariel Sharon, among other Israelis, had responsibility for the massacre.

The commission's report stated, "It is our view that responsibility is to be imputed to the Minister of Defense for having disregarded the danger of acts of vengeance and bloodshed by the Phalangists against the population of the refugee camps and having failed to take this danger into account when he decided to have the Phalangists enter the camps. In addition, responsibility is to be imputed to the Minister of Defense for not ordering appropriate measures for preventing or reducing the danger of massacre as a condition for the Phalangists' entry into the camps. These blunders constitute the non-fulfillment of a duty with which the defense minister was charged."

Sharon refused to resign.

Finally, on February 14, 1983, he was relieved of his duties as defense minister, though he remained in the cabinet as minister without a portfolio. Sharon's career was in eclipses, but he continued to burnish his credentials as a Likud ultra. Sharon has always been against any peace deal unless on terms entirely impossible for Palestinians to accept.

According to Nehemia Strasler (Ha'aretz, January 18, 2001), Back in 1979, as a member of Begin's cabinet, Sharon voted against a peace treaty with Egypt. In 1985, he voted against the withdrawal of Israeli troops to the so-called security zone in Southern Lebanon. In 1991, he opposed Israel's participation in the Madrid peace conference. In 1993, he voted "No" in the Knesset on the Oslo agreement. The following year, he abstained in the Knesset on a vote over a peace treaty with Jordan. He voted against the Hebron agreement in 1997 and objected to how the withdrawal from southern Lebanon was conducted.

As Begin's minister of agriculture in the late 1970s, Sharon established many West Bank settlements that are now a major obstruction to any peace deal. His present position is "Not another square inch of land for Palestinians on the West Bank."

Sharon will agree to a Palestinian state on the existing areas presently under either total or partial Palestinian control, amounting to merely 42 percent of the West Bank. Israel will retain control of the highways and water resources across the West Bank. All settlements will stay in place with access to them by the IDF. Jerusalem will remain under Israeli sovereignty, and he plans to continue building around the city. The Golan Heights would remain under Israel's control.

It can be strongly argued that Sharon represents the long-term policy of all Israeli governments without any obscuring fluff or verbal embroidery. For example, Ben-Gurion approved the terror missions of Unit 101. Every Israeli government has condoned settlements and buildings around Jerusalem.

It was Labor's Ehud Barak who approved the military escort for Sharon on his provocative sortie that sparked the second Intifada, and Barak who has overseen the lethal military repression of recent months. But that does not diminish Sharon's sinister shadow across the past half-century. That shadow is better evoked by Palestinians and Lebanese grieving for the dead, the maimed, the displaced, or by a young Israeli woman, Ilil Komey, sixteen, who confronted Sharon before the "elections" that brought Sharon to power as Prime Minister and leader of the Likud, when he visited her agricultural high school outside Beersheba.

"You sent my father into Lebanon," Ilil said. "Ariel Sharon, I accuse you of having made me suffer for sixteen-odd years. I accuse you of having made my father suffer for over siteen years. I accuse you of a lot of things that made a lot of people suffer in this country. I do not think that you can now be elected as prime minister."

Sharon was indeed "elected" Prime Minister of Israel, and true to his ghoulish, blood-soaked history, he continues to slaughter, destroy, and torment the Palestinian people. His policy of death, murder, and oppression has earned him the titles of "Man of Peace" and "Visionary" from George W. Bush and "Butcher of Beirut" from the rest of the world's people.

Olive trees, Oum Kulthoum, and Jasmine Blossoms

In my home, sitting in front of a picture window, facing an easterly direction to catch the morning sun, I have two small Palestinian olive trees growing in gold and green ceramic planters. I will not go into detail about how I managed to get these two small cuttings out of Palestine, but that is where they came from!

At first, when the fragile trees finally arrived from their long journey, I was not sure they would survive, but as soon as they arrived, I ran out and purchased two gold and green ceramic planters and quickly transplanted young trees in them with fresh soil and pebbles I mixed.

For the first few weeks, the olive trees did not look like they would make it. The leaves started to wilt, then began to fall off the tender little branches. I did not know what to do except to ensure they had enough water and sunlight. I even called back home to Palestine for advice and was told to put them in a place where the morning sun could get to them.

And so, like the Muslims who pray, facing the east, my Palestinian olive trees were soon facing the east, toward the land of their birth, in Palestine.

After a few weeks of the trees sitting in front of the big picture window in our living room, I noticed the trees were beginning to look healthier. The leaves stopped falling off, and shortly after that, much to my delight, I saw new growth emerging!

I was like the "proud doting father" as I tended to my "babies."

My wife and children were now beginning to tease and harass me about the way I paid so much attention to the little "refugees" from Palestine! I could swear that the more Arabic music we played at home, particularly Oum Kalthoum, Abdel Haleem Hafez, and Fairuz, the faster these little guys seemed to grow.

Now, nearly ten months later, the little olive trees are healthy and vibrant, almost tripling in size, with beautiful shiny leaves.

I sat there for nearly two hours, reflecting, thinking, and most of all, remembering… Remembering my childhood, the war, my village, our trips to Jerusalem, remembering Palestine!

Like the olive trees in my home in America when I placed them in front of the window, facing east, I too experienced a "new growth and appreciation" of my homeland, of its earth, rocks, trees, and the scent of delicate Jasmine tree's blossoms, carried by the cool afternoon breeze through an ancient hand-built home in Palestine, while the Great Lady from Egypt sang, "a thousand and one night"!

Blocking Out the Sun

My Palestinian mother has a favorite expression that she likes to use. Whenever she wanted the curtains pulled back, a window or door opened to the outside world or wanted to get out of the house to be outdoors, she would always say, *"biddy ashoof wijih rabie"* (translated: to see the face of my God).

To my mother, the "face of God" meant the beauty of God's creation, visible to all! The blue skies, the green hills, the moonlit nights, and the dew-covered flowers were all symbolic of the face of God, meant to be seen and enjoyed.

Last summer, while my family and I were in Palestine, we got to see and experience firsthand the magnificence of God's face and the ugly face of occupation and oppression, the Apartheid Wall Israel was building.

Even as a small child, I was enthralled by the simple yet awe-inspiring natural beauty surrounding me. The ancient olive trees, swaying in the morning breeze or covered in a blanket of white snow, the daily display of exquisite sunsets as the sun dipped below the surrounding hills, and my favorite, the magnificent moonlit nights when the moon first appeared to be resting on top of the hills, as if it were a giant spotlight, and then arc across the sky, saturating the entire countryside in its silver hue.

A few weeks back, I was talking on the phone with a friend who lives in the neighboring village of Al-Ram. While we were talking, he quipped that it gets darker much earlier in his neighborhood in Al-Ram than in the other areas. I laughed it off, thinking he was making another of his wisecracks, but he assured me he was dead serious.

I told to him I had no idea what the hell he was talking about and asked him for an explanation.

This is what he had to say:

His home and place of business in al-Ram, located on the main road between Jerusalem and Ramallah, faced due west. This used to be a blessing because he could sit on his porch in the late afternoons, drink a cup of tea, and smoke a cigarette as he watched the sun sink slowly behind the hills, affording him a front-row seat, perfect for enjoying the lovely sunsets.

This, he informed me, has come to an end with the building of the abominable 30-foot-high concrete wall that runs right down the middle of the main street, which connects Jerusalem to Ramallah and beyond. The wall runs the length of the road in a north-to-south direction. So, as the sun begins to set, it does get darker earlier for those people who have homes and businesses in the "shadow of the wall" because the wall blocks out the sun as it sets in the late afternoon and early evening, casting a dark shadow on them.

And so, my friend says that he will no longer sit on his porch, much as he had done for many years, enjoying the sunsets. The accursed Wall is all he sees nowadays out his windows or doors. He no longer sees *"wijih rabbou"* (the face of his God) when he looks out his door. Instead, he sees *"wijih althulum"* (the face of oppression) and the ugly shadow it casts… God's beauty, replaced by the ugliness of man!

Nakba and Memories

May 15th. 2009 - The 61st anniversary of Nakba: the disaster of the people of Palestine. On this date, May 15th, 1948, we, the people of Palestine, began our long and painful journey into exile. Dispossessed from home and homeland, this was the start of the refugee 'problem' that still exists today. More than 3 million Palestinians live as refugees in squalid conditions in camps in Palestine and throughout the Arab world.

I sat this week watching old black-and-white films of my people as they fled their homes, clutching children and what few possessions they could carry. I could not help but realize that there, but for the grace of God, could easily have been my family. But I, it seems, have a different fate and responsibility: to tell our story and document it so that it may never be forgotten.

Shortly after the June 1967 War began, the people of our village, Beit Hanina, realized the grim reality that the Israeli army would be coming here. The realization brought panic; people began to prepare to flee their homes. With memories of the atrocities of Deir Yassin and other Palestinian villages still vivid in their minds, they feared that massacres might once more be carried out. The gruesome stories of death and murder were known by all Palestinians, indeed, by all in the world who chose to know them.

Against this backdrop, my mother decided to join our neighbors as they fled with their families to the surrounding caves in the hills overlooking our village. I recall my mother frantically trying to gather what she thought we would need and could manage to carry.

She instructed me to go across our village and get my oldest sister, Aziza, who married for a year, had given birth to her first child, a son, on May 20th, 1967. Running as fast as a six-year-old could, I relayed the message to her house. My sister instructed me to tell Mom that she would follow us, with her husband, as soon as they could gather a few belongings.

I returned home and assured my mother that Aziza and her family would join us soon.

Meanwhile, my mom decided that my second sister, Najah, a thirteen-year-old beauty with long blonde hair and striking blue eyes, must be made to look like a boy. She feared for my sister's safety if the Israeli soldiers should happen to come upon us. Grabbing a pair of scissors, she chopped away at that long, beautiful hair then tossed some of my brother Musa's clothes to wear. There! Now, she looked just like a boy.

When my sister, her husband, and her infant son arrived shortly before sunset, we took what we could carry and ran to the hills. After a long and arduous climb, we made our way to a large cave whose opening faced Jerusalem, providing a vantage point for viewing the battle raging in the distance.

Inside the cave, there were about seventeen people, mostly women and children. We brought in our belongings and settled into a niche of the cave. Then, I made my way to the cave's mouth and sat down to watch the "fireworks show" lighting the night sky. Fear and anxiety could be seen on all the faces of the adults inside, but the only noise was the crying of my infant nephew and the muffled weeping of the women who pondered our fate. We had left our homes and all we had behind, and now we were sharing our fate in a cave infested with snakes and scorpions.

Around midnight, when we had been in the cave for about four hours, my mother noticed an Israeli jet circling and buzzing the area, lit by a bright, full moon. After a few more passes over our heads, my mom instructed us to gather our belongings and get out of the cave.

Others pleaded with her, trying to convince her to stay: if she left in the full moon, she would be inviting the slaughter of her children. But my mother refused to listen and grabbing me by the hand and walking with me away from the cave to a large olive tree fifty meters away.

My mother called out to those still in the cave, begging them to join us; she feared the Israeli jet was about to strike. Slowly, they began to leave the cave and joined us under the olive trees.

Just then, the jet reappeared. It made two passes, and then, on the third, it fired two missiles into the mouth of the cave. The explosion and light were beyond anything I had ever imagined; the ball of fire that blew out of the mouth of the cave was so terrifying I still hear it today. I realized that had we not listened to my mother; we would have been blown to bits in the cave.

We waited under the olive trees for about an hour lest the jet returned. Eventually, we headed to the other side of the mountain to seek another cave. We found one whose mouth faced straight up to the sky. Once inside, one could go deeper in any direction.

A child of six, I was no stranger to the caves surrounding my village. None of the children were. We had spent glorious days playing there: flying kites, tagging along as the older boys hunted pheasants, climbing in the olive trees, and eating the succulent grapes from the vines around.

After a couple of days, the hunger and thirst began to set in. There were twenty people in the cave; there was not enough food or water for everyone.

My mom would sneak into the wheat fields and cut bunches of wheat stalks, still green, in mid-June. She brought back the stalks and roasted their soft, green grains over an open fire, then rubbed them together to make the roasted grains fall out so she could give us the grains to eat.

Hunger helps enrich the memory of the food we eat for a long time. I remember the taste of that grain to this day. (Author's note: Roasting green grain is still practiced throughout much of the Arab world. The grain is roasted and cracked before being cooked in a soup called "freaka," usually with lamb or chicken.)

Today, I cannot help being mindful that we Palestinians have our own experiences with the unleavened bread — as is celebrated by the Jews who commemorate their exodus and freedom from Pharaoh. Except, of course, we commemorate our exodus and entry into the Diaspora.

The Palestinian women, anxious to feed their children, would slip into nearby abandoned homes looking for food to feed us. Once they returned with flour, water, sugar, and olive oil. They kneaded the dough and immediately baked it over a fire covered with the metal lid of a barrel, the lid providing the surface upon which the bread was baked: there was no time to wait for the dough to rise.

As an adult sharing the Jewish holiday of Passover with my friends, I am drawn by powerful but ironic parallels between the Palestinian experience of running away in fear into the wilderness, chased by an army, looking for freedom, and eating unleavened bread as we ran. For me, Pharaoh's army was the Israel Defense Forces, and we, the Palestinians, were the persecuted Jews.

Not 42 years, but a mere ten days had elapsed since we were forced to flee our homes. Still wearing the same clothes, the clothes we had left with, and having no bath since we fled, our situation was becoming quite desperate: there was no food or water. What little water we were able to get from the nearby wells was dangerously costly; some of the men had been shot and killed trying to draw water from those wells.

Most people staying with us in the cave began to speak of heading to Jordan, about 30 Km to the east. We had heard that the Israelis were offering 'safe passage' to Palestinians fleeing to Jordan. Indeed, the policy of the Israeli government was to 'facilitate' the movement of Palestinians into Jordan.

My grandfather, uncles, and their families had all made their way to Jordan; none of my mother's family had remained in Palestine. Still, my mother was hesitant to leave our home.

The entire group, we among them, left the cave early that morning in the already hot, blistering mid-June sun. We tied a white piece of cloth to a stick and marched behind it, a flag of surrender.

A neighbor, an elderly gentleman of seventy-five, took me by the hand, carefully instructing me to stay with him. If the Israeli soldiers came for him, I was to start crying and tell them he was my grandfather. He could barely walk without the aid of a cane. I clung to his hand and helped him walk the entire way.

We headed east to Jericho and Jordan. About six kilometers into our journey, we came across an abandoned home. The residents had left in a hurry, for the door was wide open.

One of the ladies went inside and returned a few minutes later with dried loaves of bread, several days old. My mom took a piece from her and gave it to me to eat. She then went to the remains of the vegetable garden and cut some green onions for me to eat with my stale bread. I had one hell of a time trying to swallow that mixture of green onions and stale bread, but my mother noticed and offered me a sip of precious water to help it down.

The sights and smells that greeted this six-year-old boy as we made our way toward Jordan can never be forgotten: the bullet-riddled bodies of Palestinian fighters, Jordanian soldiers, and Palestinian civilians, mostly women and young children, and the putrid stench of the decaying bodies bloated by the hot June sun.

I noticed some medical personnel wearing masks drenched in perfume, trying to bury some of the bodies. My mom urged me not to look to keep walking, but I could not obey; death and destruction were all around, and sometimes, I still see these images in my sleep.

We walked for another three hours, and suddenly, my mom stopped. She told us we would head back and that she feared if we did get to Jordan, we would never be allowed to return home. There was no one to help us in Jordan. Our only option would be a refugee camp. My mom refused the prospect of condemning her family to a refugee camp for the rest of their lives.

Against all the protestations of our fellow refugees, my mother turned us around and headed back to Beit Hanina. The others tried to tell her that she would get herself and her children killed, but she would not hear any of it.

About half of the people with us joined her lead and headed back into Palestine. The rest joined the long, steady stream of refugees headed for Jordan: parents carrying children, men carrying the elderly, poor people clutching their meager belongings. We were human beings in great pain, trekking in fear and in search of sanctuary. Most were never allowed to return to their homes in Palestine. Some managed to sneak back, but most became refugees in Jordan. My aunt and uncles were among those stranded in Jordan.

The pictures of the "humane" Israeli army helping people across the Allenby Bridge into Jordan made great propaganda: the Israeli soldiers carried children across collapsed bridges — an immensely powerful image for the world to see. I, too, see them helping the poor Palestinian refugees flee, but I also notice the intent of the Israeli government –which was fully aware their job was to maximize the number of Palestinians "ethnically cleansed" from Palestine by helping them to cross over into Jordan.

The Israeli government had no intention of ever allowing Palestinians to return to their homes. The Israeli soldiers were not performing humanitarian aid to refugees; they were carrying out the orders to transfer Palestinians out of Palestine. They were merely expediting the departure of the Palestinians and getting good press from it at the same time.

This past year, 42 years later, the world is again witnessing refugees on the move in Palestine and elsewhere. The suffering and injustices committed against the Palestinians go on unabated. The pain and anger have resurfaced as if they had never died: old wounds not yet allowed healing.

In Gaza today, Palestinians (most of whom are the same refugees and their descendants brutally expelled from their ancestral homes and lands in 1948) are being blockaded and starved, with the acquiescence of both the Arab world and the world at large, as the Zionist try to finish what they started in 1948.

Ramadan Memories

The Holy Month of Ramadan is again upon us, and it is time for fasting. Muslims will fast from sun-up till sundown, abstaining from food, water, and intimate relationships.

Each year around this time, my thoughts are of Ramadan in our small village of Beit Hanina, a suburb of Jerusalem that was still without electricity, where people carried lanterns to light their way in the darkness as they went first to the mosque and from there to visit friends and family; a special part of Ramadan is once again rekindled.

Beit Hanina had a drummer, charged with the pre-dawn task of awakening the village to *suhoor*, the light meal whose end marked the beginning of each day's fast. Closing my eyes and thinking really hard still brings back the sound of Beit Hanina's drummer banging away and the delightful memories of joining the other children, carrying our decorated *fanoosia* lanterns with candles burning brightly inside, as we ran along behind the drummer, singing, laughing and shouting to help awaken the sleeping adults and start them on *suhoor* and their new day. Oh, how I admired the drummer and how I wanted his job and to share his fun.

In Ramadan 1979, my first visit back to Palestine since the '67 expulsion, my cousin and I, both eighteen and living in the US, finally became the Ramadan drummers of Beit Hanina. The Israeli invasion of 1967 and the subsequent occupation made the drummers' jobs extremely considerable risk, and today they are scarce. Ramadan drummers were often stopped, even beaten, and some have been killed by the Israeli occupying army.

By 1979, Beit Hanina had not enjoyed being a drummer in five years, so my cousin and I delighted in our job of walking through the village before dawn, banging away on large tin cans. It must have been a humorous sight: the elderly were happy to hear us, the younger people thought we were a great joke and made fun of the 'bored Americans.' But everyone agreed that we had renewed some "life" that had been lost as we broke through the dark still nights of Ramadan.

I was briefly transported back to a happy childhood whose memories had never left me for a moment. I still remember sitting by the family's transistor radio with my siblings, listening to the special programs as we awaited the "cannon" to go off, signaling it was time to break our fast. The "cannon" was a World War I-era English relic and merely made a loud bang, which was all it was good for.

Ever since my children were small, I had regaled them with the many stories of my childhood in Palestine, enjoying the look of fascination as they implored me to tell them yet "another story of when you were young in Palestine."

This past summer, I took my children to visit my grandmother's grave in a hillside cemetery off Salah Eddin Street in the Old City. The cemetery is inside the boundaries of the Palestinian village of Lifta, which the Zionists ethnically cleansed of its Palestinian inhabitants, including my wife's family, in 1948. Many people, including my grandmother and her family members, are buried there, although the cemetery is now considered part of Jerusalem.

As we made our way through the cemetery gates and up the hill to read Al-Fatiha, the opening verse of the Quran, at her graveside, I noticed an old rusty cannon sitting on the top of the hill, virtually buried beneath the overgrown weeds. I decided to take a closer look. Much to my surprise, the cannon was an exact copy of the same cannon I remembered as a youth.

I called my children up the hill and showed them the cannon, surmising it was used to alert the residents of Jerusalem when to break their fast before the city fell under Zionist control.

During Ramadan, my mother invited friends and relatives to our home to break the fast with us. As Muslims, we are obligated to share breaking our fast with others, especially those less fortunate than us. It is considered a blessing to do so and a tradition we continue to honor in America. We invite friends and loved ones to share in our blessing on this Holy Month, the essence of which is a time of prayer, fasting, and charity.

Some of the best memories I carry are connected to the month of Ramadan in Palestine when I was a child. The closeness and feeling of "community" I felt during those times is almost beyond description. The sound of the drummer, the Muezzin call to prayer, the static emanating from the transistor radio, the "boom" of the cannon, the enticing aroma of the special foods we only ate during Ramadan, and the sight of families huddled together on a mat-covered floor, illuminated by the flickering light of a kerosene lantern, enjoying their meals, as humble as it may have been, in the company of family and loved ones…

These are my memories of Ramadan before the brutal Israeli invasion, which had destroyed many families and communities and is now in the process of causing further havoc as Israel continues to erect its Apartheid Walls, checkpoints, and roadblocks, reducing many

Palestinian villages and cities to nothing more than walled off ghettos and open-air prisons.

Unfortunately, these will constitute the next generation of Palestinian children's memories and experiences.

With the children of Gaza on my mind and forever in my heart.

Moonlight

As I look outside my window, I see a most beautiful full moon, so bright and brilliant, sending silver shards of light through my window shades. I remember that night in June 1967. Could the same bright, peaceful moon have lit our escape path as we ran for the neighboring hills and caves?

I remember it being so big and bright that the worn dirt path leading us away was clearly visible. The mouth of the cave faced east, and that night, the moon shone like a giant spotlight resting on top of the hill my family had owned a large chunk of for generations. The moon faced the west and looked straight into my eyes as I sat there at the mouth of the cave. I was awe-struck as the jets crisscrossed the night sky, their silvery metallic bodies gleaming and reflecting dabs of moonlight.

Could this really be war, I wondered? It did not seem like it. Except for the brilliant flashes of light later followed by the thunder, all seemed "normal."

Yes, we were cramped; more than twenty people were in the cave with us, but I had somehow tuned out all the noise of the women and the cries of the other children. That gorgeous moonlight had hypnotized me.

Suddenly, I was rudely snapped out of my hypnotic state as my mother yanked my arm, yelling for us to run away from that cave. I ran simply because of my mother's frantic yelling and urging.

We ran until we reached a large tree in the middle of an olive grove about 100 yards away. Then, I realized that my mother was still urging the others to follow. They hesitated at first but finally relented as it became clear, those jets gleaming in the moonlight, were preparing to hit us.

Not five minutes later, I saw them again, flying low overhead. After two passes, a jet positioned itself and dove at us from the east, in the same direction as that brilliant moonlight. The flash from under its wing deployed its rockets directly into the mouth of the cave where we had taken refuge only a few minutes before. There were powerful explosions as debris flew outward.

I finally realized, indeed, that this was war: a word and a reality that had carried no tangible meaning for me until that moment.

There was no electricity in my village of Beit Hanina, so I never watched TV or ever watched a movie. All I knew of war were the tales the older people talked about their experiences in 1948 and the raids by IDF into neighboring villages. Now, a first-hand experience put war into my life in bright, vivid colors, accompanied by a violently booming soundtrack.

My introduction to war was also the end of my childhood innocence. The sights and experiences that followed would be recorded by my brain for eternity, no matter how horrible they were.

The moon continued to light our way as we went through the olive groves, seeking yet another scorpion-infested cave. That cave would be our "home" for the next ten days or so. Our new 'home' opened directly overhead, looking into the sky, so I no longer had a view of the moon or what was happening around us. The only reminder of war was the ever-present thunder of the artillery in the background and the confinement of the cave.

To this day, when I look at a full moon, I wonder if it remembers that six-year-old boy gripped then, as now, in its hypnotic powers on that fateful night in early June of 1967.

Thinking of spring in Palestine

What benefit or joy if,
I was to gain the world,
But lose the almond blossoms in my land?
Drink a cup of coffee everyplace
But my mother's home
Journey to the moon,
But not to the graves of my ancestors
See the world's wonders,
But not the setting sun as it dips behind ancient olive groves
Tour the world over,
But lose the flowers on the hills of my native land
Nothing but lethal silence…
No need to gain the world
Just a cup of coffee
In a familiar place and
An end to the lethal silence
Within the hearts of the living…

MishMish (Apricots) & Palestine

Have you ever tasted something so good and special that the taste continued to linger in your memories for the rest of your life? And that no matter how many times you try, you can never duplicate it?

The memories of my childhood and my family's fruit orchards in Palestine are still as fresh today as they were when I was there as a young boy. My family's orchard produced an assortment of God's beautiful bounty. We grew olives, peaches, figs, a variety of plums, and the world's best apricots.

My favorite fruit had always been the golden, slightly blushing, sun-kissed apricots that grew on the trees my grandfather had planted decades before. These aged trees continued to produce fruit that we ate and sold to the neighboring townspeople and in Jerusalem.

I remember getting up early in the early summer mornings and running to the dew-covered orchards. I would go directly to my favorite apricot tree and pick the cool, dew-covered fruit that had fallen to the ground that morning. These slightly bruised golden beauties were absolutely the best-tasting fruit the tree offered, for they had been left on the vine to reach the peak of flavor ripeness.

The point of getting there early was two-fold. I would get there before the birds had a chance to devour the fruit as it lay on the ground, and it was nice and cool in the mornings. Since Palestine gets no rainfall in the summer, the principal water source for the trees and plants is the cool dew that blankets the area in the mornings.

I would scan the ground for the best-looking fruit, pick it up, and lift it over my mouth. I would then squeeze the golden nectar from the fruit and let it drop into my mouth. The taste of that sweet, cool nectar from the fruit is well beyond explanation. It must be experienced, for no explanation or imagery can do it justice or come close to conveying the flavor and the feeling.

The trees that produced such delicious beauty were planted by hand on land that had been in my family for hundreds of years. The hands of my ancestors worked the soil that these trees lived off of before me. Their sweat and tears were part of the soil and translated into the sweet taste I now enjoy. This was not lost on me, even as a child. For every bite we took from the bounty of our land, we thanked God and said a prayer for the people who made it possible.

I have been away from my land and country for over thirty-three years. I have been back "home" to Palestine on numerous occasions, but never in the peak season when the apricots were ripe.

Here in the US, they grow apricots as well. I even make treks to orchards to replicate the tastes and feelings I have in my memory, but to no avail. It is *not* the same. Not even close.

The tastes, smells, and experiences of my childhood in Palestine continue to haunt and taunt me. It is like an elusive love that is experienced and then lost. One can spend a lifetime trying to find and bring it back. I will cherish the taste and smell of the nectar as it dripped from the apricot till my death. It is the essence of my life and attachment to a land that was stolen from my people and continues to be.

For as long as I can remember the taste and smell of the bounty that my land and country produced, I will always yearn and dream of my return there. That is why I am deeply saddened and outraged when I see pictures of olive groves and orchards being destroyed and uprooted by Israeli bulldozers. They are more than just trees…they are much more than most Israelis and their soldiers will ever realize or know.

And on her death bed, she asked for her favorite fruit, the blushing apricot, whose season in her native village in Palestine is very brief, vanishing in a blink of an eye, and so to the market we went and purchased some apricots and presented them to her, and after just a tiny bite, she threw it down in disgust and said, "This apricot is not our apricot."

Eid al-Fitr

This piece was originally published in the Philadelphia Inquirer in 2003. Other publications picked up it and translated it into four different languages, including Hebrew. Much venom was spewed my way via e-mail by the Zionists and the pro-Israel mob when this piece was published. The Philadelphia Inquirer also got a lot of grief. Below is the entire article (with minor editing).

With the approach of Eid al-Fitr, the end of the Holy Month of Ramadan, and its fasting, I am reminded of the holidays and celebrations of my childhood in Palestine, of how eagerly we awaited Eid, its festivities, and rituals.

The nights of Ramadan leading up to Eid were spent at the mosque in prayer and reading from the Quran. Our small village of Beit Hanina, a suburb of Jerusalem, was still without electricity, and people carried lanterns to light their way in the darkness as they went first to the mosque and from there to visit friends and family, a special part of Ramadan.

Beit Hanina had a drummer, charged with the pre-dawn task of awakening the village to *suhoor*, the light meal whose end marked the beginning of each day's fast. Closing my eyes and thinking really hard still brings back the sound of Beit Hanina's drummer banging away and the delightful memories of joining the other children, carrying our decorated *fanoosia* lanterns with candles burning brightly inside, as we ran along behind the drummer, singing, laughing, and shouting to help awaken the sleeping adults and start them on *suhoor* and their new day. Oh, how I admired the drummer and how I wanted his job and to share his fun.

In Ramadan 1979, my first visit back to Palestine since the '67 expulsion, my cousin and I were eighteen and living in the US, and we finally became the Ramadan drummers of Beit Hanina. The Israeli invasion of 1967 and the subsequent occupation made the drummers' jobs extremely substantial risk, and today, and they are scarce: Ramadan drummers were often stopped, even beaten.

By 1979, the village had not enjoyed a drummer in five years, so my cousin and I delighted in our job of walking through the village each morning banging on large tin cans.

It must have been a humorous sight: the elderly were happy to hear us; the younger people thought we were a great joke and made fun of the 'bored Americans.' But everyone agreed that we had renewed some "life" that had been lost as we broke through the dark still nights of Ramadan. For me, however briefly, I was transported back to a happy childhood whose memories had never left me for a moment.

Beit Hanina's mosque was squarely in the center of the village, its majestic minaret dominating the landscape. Our muezzin, Sheikh Yameen, called people to pray from the lofty heights of the minaret. The Sheikh was blind and long past fifty, but he still made his way from his home on the outskirts of the village to the mosque independently and climbed the snaking, narrow stairs to the top of the minaret.

With only the strength of his voice, he sang the call to prayer five times a day. The Sheikh's voice was elegant and soothing; it made the call reassuring and comforting. Wherever I was, that distinctive, rich voice echoed into my ears five times a day. It still anchors me to the heart and soul of Beit Hanina.

Just before Ramadan 1968, the villagers collected funds from former residents now in the Diaspora to purchase a diesel generator to light the mosque and ease the Sheik's job with loudspeakers. Sheik Yameen's voice boomed louder and more beautiful than ever, but he no longer had to climb the minaret's stairs.

The blind Sheik loved to joke that the new lights made it easier for him to "see."

The first night the generator was used, the village was electric with excitement at the beauty of the glowing minaret that compensated for the offensive noise of the generator, which soon taught us that prayer time was approaching by the roar of it kicking into action. The minaret became a beacon of light seen from afar, lighting the area, watching us, and watching over us all.

One of the first things I did in 1979 was climb to the top of the minaret and walk around its circular balcony, taking in the awesome sight of my home, my village, and the surrounding orchards and hills. I easily traveled back to my childhood mind, realizing a long-held dream of getting a bird's eye view of my world, now marred by the eyesore of the Israeli settlements built on the land stolen from our village in 1977. Now, despite the pleas and angry protests of Beit Hanina's residents, those settlements encircle and nearly strangle my ancestral home.

As young children, we were filled with excitement at the approach of our holiday—the night before Eid al-Fitr was spent in the mosque at prayer.

The morning of Eid is a time for dressing in our holiday best and returning to the mosque for the special Eid prayers. After the prayers were finished, kisses, hugs, and handshakes peppered the joyful greetings of *"Kul Sana wa intum bekheir"* (May every year find you well) and Eid Mubarak.

The women had spent the night making all manner of special Eid sweets, and they now brought these to the mosque to share with the community.

Afterward, everyone headed to the village cemetery, walking together and visiting the graves of departed relatives. The women handed out their wonderful sweets as we recited Al Fatiha, the opening verse from the Quran. At once, we remembered our departed loved ones and enjoyed the sweets from our relatives, neighbors, and friends who were still very much with us.

This ritual is still practiced today in the overcrowded cemeteries filled with Palestinian men, women, and children who have died at the hands of the brutal Israeli occupation and oppression of the Palestinian people. The pain and sorrow on the faces of mothers, fathers, brothers, sisters, sons, and daughters are beyond description. Israel's occupation has claimed the lives of more than 2,800 Palestinians, including more than 400 children, in the past three years.

After the visit to the cemetery, the men visited the homes of their female relatives, bringing gifts of money and lingering there to drink coffee or tea and eat more sweets before eventually moving on to the next house.

The first time I was allowed to tag along with my older brothers as they made the rounds with the other men, I was overjoyed to be one of the "men."

The village comes alive with people going from one house to the next, sharing warm greetings and camaraderie as they pass one another in the streets and on the hills. Every house extends an invitation to come in and have something to eat and drink—so it was in all the small villages of Palestine.

For the children, the best part was the presents and small coins we received as gifts. We would take our money and run to the center of the village where the butcher shop (usually bustling with people buying fresh meat for the Eid feast), a couple of coffeehouses, a barber shop (busiest just before Eid), and a couple of small grocery stores were huddled together.

We rushed to buy balloons, candy, and sparklers, helping to fill the village square with laughter and noisy children playing and bragging about what they had received for Eid: marbles and spinning tops were the preferred gifts at night; sparklers helped us find our way through dark streets. We were children enjoying the simple pleasures of the holidays as only children can.

My most memorable present was the bicycle I received on Eid of 1968. That shiny red bike was the envy of every boy who gathered behind the mosque. On that first day, I refused to ride it because I did not want to get it dirty.

My last Eid at home was in 1969.

Today, as I see the painful images of my people caged in their homes by the brutal curfews, living in tents after their homes are demolished (over 1,000 demolitions in Palestine this year alone, leaving many thousands homeless), mourning the loss of loved ones, and unable to partake in even the simplest part of the Eid, I am saddened but also angered. The joy has been sucked from the lives of my people, and worse, the hope and happiness has been stolen from our children.

There is no joy to be found in mothers mourning beside the grave of their child. What delight can be found locked under curfew, forced to remain inside the home for days on end, unable to step outside for air or a loaf of bread?

At the height of Eid, a visit to Jerusalem's Al Aqsa Mosque is now forbidden to most Palestinians who have not been allowed to enter Jerusalem sometimes for five years or more. How does one celebrate the sounds of children weeping from hunger and thirst?

Lest we forget the brave and noble people of Gaza, who are not only confined to the world's largest open-air prison but are being starved and blockaded as a *policy* in the ultimate act of cruelty by Israel and her allies, Arab and otherwise, who have no shame or even a shred of morality!

This year, for Palestinians, at home and beyond, Eid will be a most somber one. The people of Palestine are foremost in my thoughts and prayers, together with all those who suffer injustice.

May the next Eid we celebrate be in FREEDOM AND PEACE.

Next year, in PEACE, in FREEDOM, in JERUSALEM. Inshallah.

May peace and happiness be the hallmark of all your holidays and celebrations. May the Holy Land know true peace, freedom, and justice for its people. May the tears of grief shed today be the last. May the only tears be of joy, life, and happiness. Amen.

Oh, Little Town of Bethlehem

This article was originally published in Newspapers on December 3rd, 2003. It is reprinted here with minor edits.

Christmas is fast approaching, and with it, the celebration of the birth of Jesus (pbuh: peace be upon him) will be enjoyed as more than one billion Christians around the globe gather with family and friends in prayer, joy, and reflection.

Children will eagerly await the morning of that blessed day with anticipation that only a child can enjoy. Christmas trees are dressed in new and old decorations for that grand day. Festively wrapped gifts will tease children to guess their contents; children will not sleep much the night before – with all those gifts begging for attention. The birth of the baby Jesus (pbuh) will be told and retold thousands of times; scenes of the Nativity and symbols of the humble birth are recreated in many forms on lawns, mantles, and endless displays. Christmas pageants and concerts will commemorate the blessed event in time-honored fashion around the world.

As a Muslim, I, too, participated in the beautiful festivals of Christmas. During elementary school in the United States, I sang carols with the school choir, performed in concerts, and joined the annual visit to Dearborn's historic Greenfield Village, which depicts American life in centuries gone by and houses a museum, historical buildings and homes that once belonged to famous Americans.

One of my favorite Carols, since early childhood, has always been 'Silent Night,' for it carries a pertinent message that sums up the atmosphere at the time of Christ's birth and reflects the true spirit of Christmas.

While I happily participated in these activities, it always seemed that my teachers and the world did all they could to deny the Palestinian connection to this blessed holiday.

I am Palestinian. I was born in Jerusalem, a few miles from Bethlehem, the Palestinian village of Jesus's birth. Singing to people with no knowledge of Palestine, Palestinians, and our link to Bethlehem and Jesus always seemed very strange. It still seems strange.

For our audiences, it was always about Israel. Repeatedly, I heard people say how nice it would be to visit the Israeli town of Bethlehem, ignoring the fact that Bethlehem is a Palestinian town and Palestinian Christians and Muslims live there under the brutal military occupation of Israel.

I soon realized that we were singing 'O Little Town of Bethlehem' to people who had absolutely no idea of what really was happening there. We were singing to people who were completely ignorant of the thousands of desperate refugees who live in Bethlehem's refugee camps. To our audience, Bethlehem was an idyllic scene often found on postcards and Christmas greetings. I knew the truth: Bethlehem is home to some of the poorest people on earth.

Palestinians, whose homes are in the refugee camps of Bethlehem, live in abject poverty and misery, as they have done for generations after being expelled from their homes with the creation of the state of Israel in the ethnic cleansing that took place in 1948. How very fitting that Holy Mary, seeking refuge from the Roman army, a safe place to give birth, came to this town.

Today, two thousand years later, Bethlehem, like much of Palestine, continues to be home to thousands of refugees. Ringed by settlements for Jews only, walled off and separated, Bethlehem today is virtually cut off from the rest of Palestine: choked by the settlements that surround her and ringed by a concrete wall. It is land, water, and other resources were expropriated by the Israelis in a relentless effort to make life even more unbearable for the Palestinian natives and refugees who call the village home.

It is inconceivable that currently, we hear of pregnant Palestinian women who must endure the hell of the Israeli occupation, its inhumane and degrading checkpoints, to reach the haven of a hospital to give birth to their children. While the Blessed Virgin found refuge in a humble stable, many of her contemporary young mothers-to-be are forced to stand endless hours at checkpoints operated by Israel's teenage soldiers who not only lack compassion but simply could not care less about the plight of a woman in labor.

Many Palestinian women have given birth in taxis or in the streets that are choked with dust in summer and swimming with mud in winter as they wait at checkpoints for hours to receive permission from the young soldier who arbitrarily decides whether they 'look pregnant or only fat.' Too many children and mothers have died from lack of medical care and failure to be allowed to pass in a timely manner.

The always 'thoughtful' and 'humane' Israeli army has gone as far as to issue 'birthing kits' to the young soldiers that control the many checkpoints that choke the life of Palestine and its people. These 'birthing kits' are to be used to help women who 'choose' to give birth at these checkpoints—no woman would opt to give birth under such conditions. Still, an ever-growing number of Palestinian infants carry the name 'Hajez' (from the Arabic word for check point) as a bitter reminder of their birthplace.

I fail to grasp what benefit such inhumanity bestows upon the Jewish state. The bitter truth is that 2,000 years after Mary gave birth to Jesus under Roman occupation, Palestinian mothers in Bethlehem and elsewhere in occupied Palestine still seek safe refuge to deliver their infants.

The birth of a human being is a momentous and joyous occasion for the parents, even for those who suffer the torturous nightmare, pain, and anxiety of checkpoint deliveries, but the tragedy of seeing this would-be a joyous event ending in the unbearable agony of the death of a newborn or its mother is unconscionable.

So, as you hear 'O Little Town of Bethlehem' this Christmas season, please pause for a moment to remember those for whom this Palestinian town is home.

Once again, there will be no Christmas festivities in Manger Square this year. The Christmas 'carols' will be a choir of Israeli tanks and helicopters pierced with echoes from the shoot-to-kill curfews that will blanket the city, not in deep and dreamless sleep, but with fear and dread; the everlasting light that shines in her darkened streets – the endless searchlights of military patrols.

The Christian children of Palestine, together with their Muslim brothers and sisters, will observe Christmas and remember its beautiful story this year, but they will have little to celebrate.

Fear and hunger will keep them awake through the night, not the anticipation of gifts and feasts as in the Christmas of other lands. While the rest of the world celebrates this glorious holiday of birth and rebirth, Bethlehem's children will pray for some brief respite from the fright of the killings, shootings, abuse, and destruction that is the reality of life in Palestine.

Picnic at al Aqsa

One of my favorite memories as a child in Palestine was when my mother (AY) used to make her scrumptious meat pies for us to eat, picnic style, on the grounds of the Al Aqsa compound in Al Quds (Jerusalem). She used to get up early in the day, prepare the dough, and take it to Al Quds (the old city) ahead of us.

Once inside the old city, she would buy her fresh ingredients of ground lamb meat, onions, parsley, and spices and take them to the old bakery in the area that she frequented and trusted. There, she would make triangle-shaped meat pies (*ikraas*), which she stuffed with her magic mixture of mouth-watering ingredients and gave pies to the baker to bake in his oven, making sure he baked them to her exacting standards of golden perfection.

Afterward, she would take the piping hot pies, the mouth-watering aroma wafting through the air, place them on a large tray, covering them with a blanket to keep them nice and warm, and meet up with us at the ground of Al Aqsa, where we would have our picnic under the shade of the ancient trees.

My mother used to make extra pies so when strangers stopped by, drawn by that intoxicating aroma, she could share it with them.

To this day, the fragrance of freshly baked bread evokes memories of my beloved late mother; may Allah have mercy on her soul and those magical moments spent with her on the holy grounds of Masjid Al Aqsa!

Letter to Elie Wiesel

A few years before he died in 2016, Elie Wiesel took out a full-page ad in the NY Times to publish his "musings" on Jerusalem in opposition to Palestinians...Below is my response, which was sent to him and the Times with minor edits.

Dear Elie Wiesel: My Response to Elie's "musings" on Jerusalem

By Mike Odetalla

Dear Elie,

I hope that you do not mind me calling you by your first name, but after reading your so-called "musings" in an expensive ad in the New York Times and other publications on the city of my birth, I feel that we can dispense with the formalities because I believe now I know you very well.

The Holy City of Jerusalem, or Al-Quds, its true and proper Arabic name, which means "The Holy," is not and has never been a "mythical" place for me; it is the city of my birth and that of my ancestors. My connection to the city is based on simple facts and truths, and not the myths, propaganda, and outright lies that seem to have permeated and corrupted the minds of the masses. While your mother may have sung you a lullaby about Jerusalem, as you claim, I took my first steps as a baby within its sacred walls on the grounds of the Al Aqsa compound. Going back to Jerusalem is a true "homecoming" for me in the truest sense of the word, even though your brethren in Israel make it as hard as humanely possible.

While you rely on ancient myths, many of which have been discredited by scholars and researchers, some of whom are Jewish, by the way, as the basis of holding my beloved city captive to the unjust and cruel whims of the racist Zionist ideology, many Palestinians still hold in their possessions the keys to the homes that they were forced to leave and have not been permitted to return to, even though that sacred right is enshrined in International Law and the laws of God himself!

When my children visit Jerusalem and Palestine, it is truly the lands of their ancestors, clear and concrete, from the graves of their forefathers to the ancient olive trees that they planted many hundreds of years before the Jewish State came to be. They do not have to rely on ancient legends to know their connection and that of their ancestors to the land. They can see, feel, and even "breathe" it!

The soil of Jerusalem and Palestine is entwined in my body, mind, and soul. It is right there where I first set foot in the Old City. I can see, smell, and taste it. Jerusalem is present in the olives and oil that I consume from my family's ancient trees, in the sweet nectar of cool, dew-covered apricot on a summer's morning, the setting sun, and the full moon that lights the hills!

You claim in your AD that "Today, for the first time in history, Jews, Christians, and Muslims all may freely worship at their shrines. Contrary to certain media reports, Jews, Christians, and Muslims ARE allowed to build their homes anywhere in the city. The anguish over Jerusalem is not about real estate but about memory."

Sir, reading that outright lie, I wonder if you really wrote that or if the Israeli Ministry of Information had, in fact, not written it for you. Either way, I cannot believe that someone like yourself, who prides himself on doing "meticulous" research, could write or lend his name to such a statement. Your "credibility" takes the hit!

The fact is that Arab Christians and Muslims are NOT free to worship at their shrines. The patently racist Israeli system of erecting concrete walls, roadblocks, and checkpoints makes it impossible for millions of indigenous Palestinian Arabs to ever reach their Holy Places. In fact, there are hundreds of thousands of Palestinian Arabs who can see Jerusalem from their homes but have a better chance of traveling to the moon than visiting the lands of their ancestors.

Also, as the facts, NOT just "certain media" reports, bear out, Palestinian Arabs are NOT permitted to "build their homes anywhere in the city." The sobering and painful fact is that Palestinian homes have been demolished by the thousands, with many more on the list threatening them with destruction. Palestinian Arabs, the rightful owners of the lands, are forced to live in cramped homes and cannot build on their OWN lands as the Zionist policies are methodically grinding on in an effort to ethnically cleanse the lands of its indigenous population.

You also claim that "Jews were not willing to kill for Jerusalem," which is an outright lie worthy of the Nazi propagandist in their heyday!

You conveniently forget about the massacres and atrocities that were committed by your Zionist brethren (I use the term "brethren" because you seem to identify with Israel and her policies as your own by spreading the myths, propaganda, and outright lies of the so-called "Jewish State") against the Palestinian Muslim and Christians whereby thousands were massacred, and hundreds of thousands were expelled from their homes, lands, and villages to create the "Jewish State."

Maybe the name Deir Yassein could stir your memory a bit, or the village of Lifta, the village of grandmother which overlooks Jerusalem and still stands with empty homes that the Zionist forces saw fit to blow holes in their roofs and floors to make them uninhabitable and to discourage their rightful owners from returning to them!

My grandmother's grave, and that of many of her relatives and fellow villagers, is but a stone's throw from Jerusalem's Damascus Gate and overlooks the ancient city walls; the golden Dome of the Rock is clearly visible, and the painful fact is that her living relatives are not even permitted to come and visit her grave site to say a simple prayer. In fact, the population of her entire village was transformed into homeless refugees, and she died yearning to return to the village of her ancestors!

You also seem oblivious to the fact that not a day goes by that the Zionist forces do not maim, kill, or destroy Palestinian life and property, and for what? Even the blind can see that the nefarious policies of the Jewish State have one and ONLY one goal: to steal as much land as possible and to make life unbearable for the Palestinian Arabs! You desire the land, BUT NOT the people that are on it, pure and simple.

No Mr. Wiesel IT IS and has always been about "real estate" when it comes to the Zionists and their plans and the only memory, they care about is one based on mythology and manufactured history, while ignoring the very REAL memories of the Palestinian Arabs as they seek to usurp not only the lands, but the memories and history of those whose roots pre-date even Judaism itself!

A few years back, a Jewish friend lamented to me that Zionism and its narrative has transformed Israel into a nation that worships not God, but rocks, trees, and soil. Your call for "putting off such a sensitive issue" is nothing more than the very policy of the racist Israeli state as it continues to devour Palestinian lands and seeks to create such "facts on the ground" that would make the return of Jerusalem to its rightful owners all but impossible! Even as your ad was going to press, the Jewish State was busy with announced plans to build yet more Jewish only colonies on stolen lands, making a mockery of your idiotic "musings" and that of International Law itself!

Instead of dwelling in the lands of myths, open your eyes to what is being done in your name in the Holy Lands. An entire people are being imprisoned and starved in the 21st Century right before your eyes, and yet all you can do is conjure thousand years old legends to justify actions and ideologies that cannot and should not be defended!

Shame on you!

Abu Ali

As Israeli bulldozers destroy more homes, trees, orchards, fields, and lives with their plows of destruction, I recall my uncle (aunt's husband) Jameel (Abu Ali) and happier, simpler times.

Abu Ali could neither read nor write; education was a luxury he could not afford.

He began working incredibly young when his father became chronically ill; Abu Ali was the oldest son. He married my aunt (my mother's sister) at an early age and soon supported his father's family and his own. Abu Ali did many back-breaking and menial jobs, but his primary income came from plowing the village orchards and fields. Together with his ever-present and trusty mule, Abu Ali made it to difficult places that still boggle my mind.

Abu Ali was a slim yet extraordinarily strong, dark man with a face turned leathery from the strength of the Palestinian summer sun, but that always carried a smile. His hands were tougher than leather and coarse as sandpaper from holding the plow all those years. His great strength came partly from the years of carrying the heavy plow everywhere he went.

The subsiding spring rains allowed the earth to dry enough for Abu Ali to begin his work in the orchards and fields each year.

His day began at daybreak and did not end until the setting of the sun. A thermos of hot tea, a jug of water for drinking and ablutions before prayer, and a handkerchief wrapping a tomato, an onion, and some olives together with a couple of loaves of my aunt's hearth-baked bread were what he took with him every morning. Dinner always awaited him at home when he finished his work.

Seeing Abu Ali making his way to the fields and orchards was soothing and reassuring to me as a boy. It meant that spring was here, and soon, the village would come to life as people began to work in their orchards.

I used to climb the hills surrounding my village and look for Abu Ali. He was not hard to spot because I could easily make out the straight lines of freshly turned earth, indicating he was hard at work. Whenever it was time for him to plow my family's land, my mother would make lunch for Abu Ali, and I would bring it to him.

God bless her; my mother always fed anyone who worked on our land. To this day, she believes that feeding one who is hungry is the least one human can do for another. I always looked forward to running whatever food my mother packed for my uncle.

Taking a break from his hard labor, he would sit in the shade of one of our olive trees and enjoy his lunch while enchanting me with stories of years gone by: our village, our people, and much, much more.

I loved Abu Ali's life so much that, one day, I informed my mother I wanted to quit school and become a *harrath* (one who plows for a living). She scolded me and told me that a *harrath* was not a good profession and that if given a chance, Abu Ali would have gone to school and gotten an education. At eight, I wanted no part of what she said. I knew if I asked my uncle, he would delight in teaching me to follow him.

One day, as we sat under a very ancient olive tree, I told him of my decision. He was, as I knew he would be, pleased and agreed to help me attain my goal.

Immediately, Abu Ali invited me to stay with him for the rest of the day, and I immediately began to learn my new profession. I could not believe my good fortune: this man would teach me his profession no matter what my mom thought or said, he would teach me to be the best *harrath* the world has ever known.

My first job was to learn to feed the mule, easy enough! Then, he told me to clean the plow. I managed, although I had never seen him do this before.

After a while, he rose and asked if I was ready to learn the trade.

"Of course!" I yelled with joy.

Abu Ali instructed me to bring five small pointy pebbles.

Not questioning my teacher, I brought the pebbles, and Abu Ali told me to hold the pebbles in my right hand and grab the plow with the same hand while keeping the pebbles safe against the plow's wooden handle.

After a few short passes with the pebbles pressing uncomfortably against my palm, the pain was more than I could bear. Indeed, I was shocked to see that my palm was bleeding lightly.

Asking permission to stop for a moment, I looked at my aching and injured little hand. Bewildered, I asked my uncle why I must hold these pebbles when I knew he plowed without them.

With a wizened smile, Abu Ali gently informed me only thus can one "toughen" his hands to endure the harsh conditions of plowing and asked me if I was ready to continue.

"Not really," I said, reconsidering this profession.

Abu Ali laughed aloud and told me to go to my mother and tell her that Abu Ali had taught me all I needed to know about plowing. Little did my young mind know to be grateful for the collaboration between my mother and Abu Ali in a very simple but important lesson that day...

Abu Ali passed away ten years ago. With his passing, we lost much more than the man who plowed our land; we lost a small part of us and our way of life.

God have mercy on his soul.

Of Passover, Exile, and Deliverance

The Jewish holiday of Passover is once again upon us...

As the Jews of the world, and particularly those who live in Israel, get ready to celebrate the Passover holiday or Pesach, I cannot help but draw an analogy between this holiday and my experience during the 1967 war.

This holiday commemorates the departure of the Israelites from Egypt. Pesach marks the birth of the Jewish people as a nation led by Moshe (Moses) over 3000 years ago. This is as much a celebration of their spiritual freedom as the physical liberation from slavery.

In their haste, the Jews had no time to let the kneaded dough sit and rise. Rushed as they were, the Israelites did not have time to bake their bread or prepare any food.

The children of Israel wrapped up their dough, leftover matzah, and bitter herbs in their clothing, placed the bundles over their shoulders, and walked joyfully out of the land of Egypt. The dough was backed by the hot sun and eaten with bitter herbs. Passover marked the freedom of the Jews from slavery...

As a child, I remember hearing tales from the elders, particularly those who became refugees, of how they were forced to flee their homes, lands, and villages, many at the point of a gun. They were forced to leave in such a hurry, taking only what they could carry and abandoning most of their belongings. Many lifetimes worth of hard work and memories were left behind in those homes and villages, which were eventually looted and destroyed deliberately and systematically by the Zionists!

As I look at the black-and-white pictures of long lines of Palestinians forced to flee their lands, I cannot help but equate Pharaoh's army with the Zionist army as they chased my people from their ancestral homes!

The Israelites made camp and began celebrating their freedom from Egypt after crossing the Red Sea, while the Palestinians were given tents and told to wait for their eventual return from their exile. More than 700,000 Palestinians were driven from their homes. Destitute and suffering from hunger and thirst, they were left to the elements; their only shelters were the flimsy tents donated by the international community!

The Mukhiamat, which means "tent cities" in Arabic, was supposed to be temporary housing for the Palestinian refugees. They were promised by the international community and the UN, through the passing of UN Resolution 194, that they would be able to return to their homes as soon as possible. In fact, as a condition for entry into the UN, the newly declared State of Israel had to agree to UN Resolution 194! More than 60 years later, the "temporary" solution to the Palestinian refugees' plight is still ongoing. The "tent cities" have grown and become squalid ghettos, and cinder block hovels with corrugated tin roofs have replaced the tents.

Today, I cannot help being mindful that we Palestinians have our own experiences with the unleavened bread – as is celebrated by the Jews who commemorate their exodus and freedom from Pharaoh. Except, of course, we commemorate our Nakba (catastrophe of being dispossessed) and entry into our own Diaspora.

The Palestinian women, including my mother, anxious to feed their children, would slip into nearby abandoned homes looking for any food to feed us.

Once, they returned with flour, water, sugar, and olive oil. They kneaded the dough and immediately baked it over a fire covered with the metal lid of a barrel, the lid providing the surface upon which the bread was baked. There was no time to wait for the dough to rise as we were in constant fear and flight as we lived in and moved from cave to cave in the surrounding hills. We ate the unleavened bread with Za'atar, a somewhat bitter herb that grows wild in the Palestinian hills.

As an adult, having shared the Jewish holiday of Passover with my friends, I am drawn by powerful but ironic parallels between the Palestinian experience of running away in fear into the wilderness, chased by an army, looking for freedom, eating unleavened bread as we ran. Pharaoh's army was the Israel Defense Forces, and we, the Palestinians, were the persecuted Jews.

I remember a meal of stale bread, which we found outside an abandoned home, and the green onions my mother pulled from the garden. She fed me this with a sip of stale water to wash it down.

While Jews in Israel celebrate their "freedom," they continue to oppress, kill, imprison, and starve others. The unleavened bread is now eaten with the leaves of organically grown lettuce, which serves as the "bitter herbs" and is grown in many Jewish-only colonies built on the stolen lands of the Palestinians.

When Jews around the world recite the traditional Passover prayer "May all those that are hungry eat," before they commence their feast, those who are truly hungry in Gaza are *not* allowed to eat due to the inhumane closures and suffocating blockades imposed on them by the Israelis! Thousands of Gazans had their homes, fields, and lives destroyed and decimated by the Israeli army, forcing them once again to brave the elements in tents while the Jews of Israel celebrate and feast. Gazans a mere few hundred yards away are being starved as if they existed in an entirely different universe.

Fleeing in fear, unleavened bread, and bitter herbs…something to think about this Passover…while the Palestinians still await their "deliverance" in hunger from modern-day Pharaoh!

Sabr (cactus) Plants

Cactus plants do not grow in "straight lines" naturally...

On one of my first visits to my home in Palestine, in 1979, since I left in 1969, we took a trip through the area that was forbidden to us until 1967, the area that became Israel after most of its inhabitants were brutally ethnically cleansed from their homes, lands, and villages. In all, more than 500 Palestinian villages were wiped out, leaving little, if any, evidence of their existence, whereby even the stones that were once part of the homes were ground up into pieces.

The Zionists wanted to make sure that nothing was left for the Palestinian residents to come back to and, at the same time, hide all evidence of their crimes in Palestine and all traces of the people that "did not exist," perpetuating the myth of "a land without a people for a people without a land."

As we drove along the highway, we passed many "open areas" that were empty, except for the Sabr (cactus) plants that dotted some of the hillsides and other areas. It was curious to see Sabr plants in certain places and not others. Why here and not there? Also, as everyone knows, Cactus plants do not naturally grow in "straight lines," yet here they were, in straight lines in the middle of "nowhere!"

These plants are a "curiosity" of nature, a "natural wonder" in Israel, as one Jew told me. He went further in his explanation and stated that cacti represented the "tenaciousness of the Jewish people and how they cling to the land" ...

Yet, I and most Palestinians know that these Sabr plants have a rather tragic and sad tale to tell. For you see, they are what is left of the hundreds of small Palestinian villages that were destroyed and depopulated. All Palestinian villages had these plants, and some used them as fences and barriers as well as a source of delicious fruit. In fact, to this day, one cannot go inside a Palestinian village and not see cactus plants in and around homes and fields.

The Sabr plant is tenacious and has survived in the harshest conditions for hundreds of years. As a child, I can remember many times getting the irritating fine thorns in my hands and fingers as I tried to pick its fruit. It is our symbol as Palestinians.

On many occasions, while traveling throughout Palestine, I stopped my car in the middle of nowhere to view these plants and their surroundings, stepping out of my car to look at these last traces of my people's villages and the lives they lived.

It was not hard to imagine what these villages might have looked like or who might have lived there. I often wondered where they are now, the people who planted and tended these plants. How is it that they should still be living in squalid refugee camps while their land awaits their return?

People who do not know this would look at me with puzzled faces. But I know these plants are a testimony and stand as silent witnesses, their secrets readily available to anyone who wants to learn the truth of the Palestinian history.

I wish these plants could talk. They would surely bring tears to the eyes of the listener with their tales of sadness and tragedy. The Sabr plants serve as a living memorial to the lives and dreams that were destroyed along with the villages.

We Palestinians are not allowed to place memorial markers like the Israelis do to show our loss and grief, but God has given us a more powerful memorial than any made by human hands. So please, next time you notice a string of Sabr plants growing in the middle of nowhere, take a moment to reflect and learn. There is a reason that it is where it is…

PS. The Israelis have taken the name Sabra to mean a Jew who was born in Israel as opposed to one who immigrated.

How ironic is it that the Sabr plants are not "native" to Palestine but were introduced from Mexico in the 1600s.

The Victim to Guarantee His Oppressor's Security

11/16/05

Hillary Clinton

Dear Hillary,

My name is Mike Odetalla. I am a Palestinian/American and a father of three, who was born in 1960 in my ancestral village of Beit Hanina, which is a suburb of Jerusalem, and according to internationally recognized laws, conventions, and resolutions, is considered part of the occupied Palestinian Territories that were invaded and captured by Israel in the 1967 war. I was a child of war, having lived through the 1967 war, whereby my mother, my siblings, and I were forced to flee our home and seek refuge in the scorpion-infested caves that populate the hills that surrounded our village.

During the first night of the war, our family and the other 20 odd women, children, and the elderly, which included my 6 days old nephew, barely escaped getting blown to bits by an Israeli fighter jet that circled overhead, its metallic body glistening under the full moon lit sky, which then proceeded to fire a missile into the mouth of the cave a mere few moments after my mother grabbed us, imploring the others in the cave to follow, as we scampered into a nearby olive grove, clinging to each other for comfort as the flash and deafening thunder of the blast rang in our years.

We spent the next 20 odd days moving from cave to cave as my mother and the other women tried to sneak back into the abandoned houses in our village, managing at times only gather flour and precious water for their children. Jews celebrate Passover by eating unleavened bread, which signifies their hurried Exodus out of Egypt whereby they took and baked the dough before it had time to rise. My mother baked our bread in the same fashion since we also did not have the luxury of waiting for the bread, as we were on the move, trying to stay one step ahead of the Israelis.

In 2002, when my American born children were old enough to fully understand and comprehend, I took them back to the hills of Beit Hanina and the to the very same caves that I huddled in with my family 35 years prior. We retraced our steps as we fled our homes in that June moonlit night, stopping in front of the cave whose mouth was destroyed by the Israeli fired missile. It was important for me to show my children and tell them of my experiences as well as the experiences of their grandparents on their mother's side who were ethnically cleansed from their homes and lands by the Zionist founders of Israel in 1948, forcing them and more than 750,000 other Palestinians to become homeless refugees, living in squalid conditions in refugee camps. Their grandparent's home in the village of Lifta still stands today, even though their grandparents are not allowed to move back, contrary to UN Resolution 194, and other internationally recognized Laws, and conventions that deal with the refugees Right of Return to their homes.

I know that these details might not be of importance to you, but they are very important to me and to the millions of other Palestinians, especially in light of your recent trip to the Holy Land, whereby you reiterated your support for the Apartheid wall that Israel has been building to imprison my people into discombobulated walled off ghettos and in the process, steal their precious lands.

You stood with your back to the concrete wall and had the audacity to say to the Palestinians people, "This wall is not against the Palestinians. This is against the terrorists. The Palestinian people must help to prevent terrorism. They must change the attitudes about terrorism." Your words proved yet again that neither you nor anyone else in our government has any grasp of reality of what is happening in the ground in Palestine. The victim is once again placed in the unenviable position of having to guarantee the security of his oppressor, while being denied his own basic human rights and security or for that matter, the freedom to of movement in his or her own town or village.

Did you really believe the words that were coming out of your mouth? Did you give thought to those words before uttering them or were you just going through the motions of being a politician, saying and doing anything to get elected without the burden of a conscience or sense of justice?

My family, as well as the residents of the village of my birth, Beit Hanina, is some of those Palestinians that you claimed the wall was not being built against. Beit Hanina, like many other Palestinian villages and cities, will be turned into a walled off ghetto, whereby families will be cut off from one another as well as their fields and orchards. The villagers of Beit Hanina, which include members of my family, will lose access to their ancestral lands which will then be confiscated by the Israelis. Did you not find it odd the way the wall snakes in and around the Palestinian built up areas, swallowing the most desirable pieces of land, while at the same time, excluding their rightful owners?

You also saw it fit to visit the Israeli settlement of Gilo, which is built on the stolen lands of the Palestinian village of Beit Jala, whereby the colonizer of the illegal settlement cheered and showered you with their affection. You reciprocated that affection by pledging your fealty to the state of Israel and her policies, no matter what the consequences of those policies were to the brutalized and maligned Palestinian people, the very same people who graciously and warmly hosted you and your husband Bill. You even accepted a hand embroidered Palestinian folk dress, which you wore with a smile on your face, glowing in the world class hospitality of the Palestinian people, the very same people that you now turn your back on, joining the right-wing chorus as you demonize them and their society.

Could you not find it in your heart to actually visit with some of the Palestinian people or were you afraid of photographs showing you with a

Palestinian child might mysteriously crop up during your future campaigns for higher office?

As the first lady of the United States, you once wrote a book with the title of "It Takes a Village" in reference to the old African proverb that it takes a village to raise a child. As you toured the Palestinian areas, did you ever once think about the children who were being trapped behind the 30-foot-high concrete wall, cutting them off from their family, friends, and access to their schools? What kind of a childhood and life will these children have as the "village" that is supposed to be their home and center of their universe is reduced to nothing more than an open-air prison.

Yes, it does indeed take a village, a global village minus the physical and mental walls which believes in the universal principles of compassion, mercy, and most of all, justice to raise a child who will grow up to realize his or her full potential as a human being...Hillary Clinton

Mike Odetalla..." A seed in the eternal fruit of Palestine."

Up A Tree...

I remember the day as if it were yesterday...

It was June 21, 1967. We had just returned home after spending nearly two weeks running and hiding in the caves surrounding our village in Palestine. The Israeli army had conquered the entire West Bank and Gaza Strip in the 6 Day war.

At the onset of the War, we were told by our fearless (pun intended) leaders that they were on the verge of victory, while they were on the verge of defeat. We were told to head for the hills and wait for the war to end in victory. We took to the hills, whole families made up mostly of women and children, with only the clothes on our backs. We took no food or water.

I remember sitting in the mouth of an ancient cave in the village mountain, looking at the bright flashes of light, followed by the loud booms. I was a child of six. I did not fathom the gravity of our situation at that precise time.

My mother had gathered us (our family consisted of myself, a 16-year-old brother, an 12-year-old sister, and my married sister, her husband, and their 14 day (about 2 weeks)-day-old baby). We ran from cave to cave, field to field, seeking food, water, and shelter. This went on from June 6, 1967, to June 20. We survived, thank God, and went back to our homes.

My mother told me not to go outside our family compound on the morning of June 21. The Israeli Army had imposed a curfew on all movement. The situation was tense, and we did not know what would happen to us. But being a curious child, I could not see myself staying put that long. The moment my mom turned her back, I climbed over the wall and made my way to one of our orchards when the apricot orchards were ripe with fruit.

I made my way through the fields and onto the main road. One of our family orchards was adjacent to the main street. My favorite climbing tree, an old apricot tree over thirty years old and about twenty-five feet high was full of ripe apricots.

I climbed higher and higher until I reached the very top and picked the best fruit to eat. I had perfect vantage of the long, winding road that snaked into our village.

Having lost myself in my special tree, I peeked over the branches, and what I saw filled me with horror. The road was filled with a long line of tanks, jeeps, and soldiers coming directly toward me. I panicked. There was no way I could climb down the tree and make it to my home without being seen—the mind of a six-year-old started playing all kinds of scenarios. I was sure I was a goner.

The column of soldiers and equipment came to a sudden stop right beside my tree.

A group of about ten soldiers climbed over the small wall and made their way directly beneath my tree. Because the tree was so large, it offered an ideal respite from the sun's heat. They decided it would be the place for them to rest and eat.

They took off their backpacks, lay underneath the tree, and proceeded to eat and talk. I was directly above their heads. I was sure that if I moved just a bit, they would discover me. This was the first time in my life I had come in any contact with an Israeli or a Jew.

I stayed crouched in that tree for almost three hours, but what seemed to me an eternity. I did not move. I tried to breathe as little as possible.

The soldiers left after the three odd hours and continued their way. They had no idea that a terrified little Palestinian boy had been perched high over their heads all that time...

After I was sure they were no longer in sight, I climbed down, my arms and legs sore and cramped, and ran home for a well-deserved scolding.

Allah works in mysterious ways

Back in November of 1989, when I was struggling and traveling all over the state and the US, setting up at sports card shows, I had a chance to set up at what was billed as one of the biggest shows in the country. The show was to be held at a new stadium built to eventually attract a major league baseball team to the St. Petersburg/Tampa Bay area.

I decided to drive from Michigan with my wife and two-year-old son and set up at the show in hopes of making some much-needed money at that time. I paid a $400 fee for two tables and another $400 for a hotel room, plus the expenses of driving the 1,200 miles (16 hours), which put me in a $1,200 hole before I even started.

The show was scheduled to run from Friday through Sunday, and I prepared my stock and even borrowed $10K from a friend to purchase sealed cases of vintage hockey cards, promising to pay him back upon my return. I even promised my wife and son I would take them to Disney World if I did well.

We arrived in Florida, and on Friday morning, I left my wife and son at the hotel and headed to the stadium to get set up. I unloaded my van and was ready for the doors to open and make some money at this nationally billed show, featuring all of the living Hall of Fame baseball players signing autographs.

On my first day, I did a whopping $100, and it soon began to dawn on me I had made a huge mistake as the crowds were more interested in getting (and paying) for autographs than buying sports cards, especially hockey and basketball cards which I specialized in.

There were huge crowds on Saturday, but again, they were not interested in buying what I was selling. I did a little over $150 for the day, and panic set in. I was mad at myself for putting my family in such a situation and did not know how I would pay my friend back the money I had borrowed, or the $1,500 credit card bill I had racked up. I was miserable and did not sleep a wink Saturday night.

On Sunday morning, we checked out early to save a bit of money. I took my wife and child to the show with me so we could leave and head home.

The show was supposed to end at 5 PM, but by 3 o'clock, I started to pack up, mad as hell, and feeling like I was carrying a 500-pound weight on my back.

As I was putting away my things, my back turned to the display, I heard a guy asking me, "What's in those cases?"

It was a question I had answered dozens of times and was in *no* mood to answer again.

As I turned, I was blinded by the huge diamond on the finger of the lady standing next to the guy, but I answered in a "not so polite" tone.

He then asked me, "How much?"

Still not in the mood, I threw out stupidly high numbers.

The man nodded and said, "I see," and walked away.

I mumbled, "Another effin a**hole," and sped up my pace of packing, wanting to get the hell out of Florida as fast as humanly possible.

I would drive straight home, not knowing how I would face my friend and the promise I made to him.

While piling my stuff on a cart, I heard the same man asking me, "What are you doing? The show is not over. Where is your stuff?"

I responded, "Why?"

He got close and said, "Well, I want to buy some things."

I was not going to unpack for anyone to spend a few dollars, so I asked him, "What are you interested in?"

He said, "All of them!"

I thought I misheard him. "All of what?"

He then pointed to the cases whose prices I had jacked up in anger.

In fifteen minutes, that man spent close to $30K, all in cash, and as I later found out, he was a very wealthy and well-known dealer of high-end boats.

Needless to say, we ended up staying a few more days in Florida, and yes, we went to Disney World...

Allah works in mysterious ways, and as Islam teaches us, if something is meant for you, you cannot escape, but if it is not, you will never find it, no matter what...

PS... Those cases of cards are now worth over $200K if he kept them sealed.

110

"Yes, yes, you call it Palestine, I call it Israel."

The biggest enemy of the Palestinian people are not the Zionist zealots (make no mistake, they are *very* dangerous), but the millions of "well-meaning" Christians who, through their ignorance, silence, and "love Arabs and Jews," not only enable the "hidden" nefarious face of Zionism but let it thrive...

Case in point:

After Friday prayers yesterday, my wife, boys, and I took my dad to a local Arabic restaurant in Dearborn for lunch. We ordered and started eating when I noticed two "American" gentlemen looking at what we were eating with interest. It seemed their curiosity was piqued by the eggplant salad we ordered.

After they were done eating, one of the gentlemen (who turned out to be an ordained minister) approached us and asked about the salad.

I told him of the ingredients and, as is my nature, scooped some into a piece of pita bread and offered it to him. He took it, ate it, thanked me, and exclaimed it to be fantastic. He also felt obliged to tell me that "I love Arabic food, and I just *love* Israel. In fact, I have been there sixteen times with my group."

I looked at him and said, "We are Palestinians *from* Jerusalem!"

He said, "Yes, yes, you call it Palestine, I call it Israel. Same place. I love it. In fact, when I am over there, I feel a certain peace, of belonging, and I cry whenever I have to leave."

His friend felt compelled to show me his "Jerusalem" hat, with the Star of David and a Menorah, as he also gushed about how much he also loved Israel, but he had only been there a handful of times and that he loved "helping the people there, Arabs and Jews."

I was then informed by the minister, who was wearing a Toledo Mud Hens cap, that his group helped the Arab Bedouins in Beersheba.

I interrupted with, "Those are the same Arab Bedouins that Israel has been trying to ethnically cleanse by destroying their homes and villages. In fact, they are doing so as we speak."

"Yes, you may be right," he retorted. "But I do not get into the Politics of it all. We go into Nazareth, Beersheba, and all of the Israeli towns to help people. Our Tour Guides, when we go to Arab towns, are "believers" (Christian Arabs) ..."

This set me off on the following rant:

"Sir, you claim to be a man of God. You say that you have been to Israel sixteen times to "help people," and yet you tell me that you have *never ever* been to *any* town in the West Bank, including the birthplace of Jesus? How could that be?

"If you are, as you claim to be, and I do not doubt your sincerity to be a follower of Jesus, then you know that he spoke for and helped the downtrodden. He stood for, first and foremost, for justice. All I ask of you is to go there and visit how the 'other half lives' with an open mind and an open heart and let your faith be your guide.

"As a Christian and as a minister, if you witness a gross injustice or a crime, can you honestly stand silent? Turn away and pretend it did not happen? If so, then you are neither a Christian nor, more importantly, a human being, sir!

"It is *not* a 'Political problem!' It is a question of basic human rights and, first and foremost, a question of Justice. All I ask of you is to walk in the footsteps of Jesus and see what the Israelis do not want you to see, and I guarantee that it will change you!

"Discard your tour guides, *especially* the Christian Arab ones they recommend to you. In Jerusalem, you will find some Christian and Muslim Arab tour guides that are not willing to abide by their master's 'script'..."

The minister promised he would and asked me when we will be at this restaurant again as I have given much to think about.

"Every Friday around this time," I replied...

The minister has been coming to this restaurant, in the heart of the largest Arab community outside the Middle East, for years, and *not once* has anyone ever engaged him...

A sad reality check for me!

Letter to Hillary Clinton

I sent this letter to then Secretary of State Hillary Clinton when it was announced that Israel was not allowing PASTA into Gaza...

Dear Hillary...Mike Odetalla a "concerned" patriot!

My letter to Hillary dated 5\5\2009...

March 5th, 2009

Dear Secretary of State Hillary Clinton,

The last time that I wrote to you, in case you might have forgotten was after your trip to Palestine in November of 2005, that letter concerned your support for Israel's Apartheid Wall and the theft of Palestinian lands, BUT that is in the past when you were just another "senator from New York".

I am now writing to you about a subject that is infinitely more important. It concerns our national security, and as an American Citizen and Patriot, it is my duty and obligation to write you after listening to and reading the remarks made by Robert Wood on February 25th during a State Department daily press briefing concerning "pasta as a dual use item".

Although I must admit my ignorance in the dual use of pasta, I am not one to question the wisdom of my democratically elected officials and their vigilance for my safety and the safety of my country, its citizens, and its interests abroad. I felt it was my duty to go out and see who is selling and buying pasta, lentils, and other items, that if gotten in the "wrong hands" (those dastardly Palestinians living in Gaza) can be spell the end of our friend, Israel and who knows, maybe with the proper preparation and quantities, will one day endanger America!

Much to my shock and dismay, my local supermarkets had vast displays of pasta piled high and being sold at one chain that I will, for national security reasons, name only after you contact me personally, at 10 for $10. That is 10 boxes of pasta for $10 and the manager informed me that he could get me as much as I wanted, possibly truckloads of this stuff (I lied to him and told him that I was planning a spaghetti dinner fund raiser at a local church).

It blew my mind that the new Obama Administration was nowhere near as vigilant as the prior Bush administration was and that the conservative pundits and talking heads were right all along when they warned us of Obama's inexperience in these "sensitive" national security matters.

My search for pasta and lentils did not end at the supermarket chains. I decided to expand my search and disguised as a "Palestinian" (I wore a black and white Keffiyeh around my neck which I learned about while searching on the internet as being the national symbol of the Palestinian struggle) I walked into one of the country's largest Middle Eastern grocery store, smack in the middle of the largest Middle Eastern community in the country, Dearborn, Michigan.

In the store I found many things that quite honestly concerned me because of the sheer volume of these items, which cannot be found in "American" supermarkets, and therefore can also have "dual usage" if you know what I mean! There in plain sight and stacked on gills were aisles full of olive oil, olives, cans of humus, rice, and would you believe it, PASTA, and LENTILS! I counted hundreds of packages of pasta and lentils on the shelves and some of them had Arabic writing on them which I could not read (obviously they were not meant for us "Americans" to read or understand). I asked one of the clerks if they had any more pasta and or lentils, and he told me that they had an entire WAREHOUSE FULL OF THE STUFF!

Imagine a Middle Eastern community with unfettered access to as much pasta and lentils as they want. The more I thought about it, the more concerned and panicked I became. I managed to buy a box of pasta, lentils, and olive oil, all with Arabic writings on them and stored safely in my garage for you to inspect and use as "evidence", but to my anger and dismay, my daughter found the box of pasta and made spaghetti for her and her brothers, used the olive oil to make salad dressing, but the lentils are still intact (she didn't know what to do with them)…

If you wish, I can go back there dressed as a Palestinian and buy all the pasta, lentils, and olive oil they have, but you will have to send me the money somehow so that I can make this purchase, and of course make sure to send me marked bills so that we have "proof".

Please contact me ASAP so that we can get these potentially dangerous items off the store shelves and by doing so, save the Jewish State from being wiped off the face of the earth via macaroni, or heaven forbid, death by rigatoni.

Also, I am worried that the Palestinians of Gaza will use lentils, which are also prohibited from entering Gaza, much in the same way that Israel uses cluster bombs by packing them into rockets and firing them at Israel towns and villages (I can imagine the horror and the billions of dollars Israel would need from the US for cleaning up the millions upon millions of tiny lentils, scattered over a vast area and the damage they would cause). No Israeli child would be safe from potentially stepping on one these deadly little kernels which would blend in with the landscape.

We must make sure that the Palestinians of Gaza never get their hands on any significant amount of pasta, lentils, and or other foodstuffs that could endanger the existence of the Jewish State which you said during your failed bid for president that you would use "any and all means to defend."

Keep Israel safe, starve the Palestinians!!!

Mike Odetalla, a "concerned American citizen"!

***

Mike Odetalla

From State Department Daily Press Briefing

February 25, 2009

>QUESTION: But can you imagine any circumstance under which pasta could be considered a dual-use item? Or is there some -- you know, is rigatoni somehow going to be used as a weapon? (Laughter.)
>
>MR. WOOD: I am not involved in those discussions, so I -
>
>QUESTION: Well, I mean -- I mean, it just seems to be absurd on the face of it, if that is what is happening.
>
>MR. WOOD: Well, there are people on the ground who are dealing with these issues. And I think we should leave it --
>
>QUESTION: Dealing with the pasta dual-use issue?
>
>QUESTION: Yes, can you take a question on the pasta, please?
>
>MR. WOOD: I am not going to take the question on the pasta --
>
>QUESTION: Why?
>
>MR. WOOD: -- because it is -
>
>QUESTION: Well, the United States is obviously pushing it, so obviously it is something --
>
>MR. WOOD: We are trying to get humanitarian supplies in - on the ground to the people in Gaza.
>
>QUESTION: Do you think food is a humanitarian supply?
>
>MR. WOOD: Food certainly is.
>
>QUESTION: All kinds of food?
>
>MR. WOOD: I - I am not able to tell you from here whether it -
>
>QUESTION: Can you get a - can you take the question of what kind of food that the U.S. thinks is a humanitarian supply?

MR. WOOD: I am not going to take that question, because I do not think it is a legitimate question.

QUESTION: You do not think it is legitimate that the Palestinians need certain foods and is - should Israel decide what food the Palestinians need?

MR. WOOD: I am sorry, Elise, I am not going to -up I have spoken on it.

This, Too, I Will Remember

This, too, I will remember...
People huddled in darkness,
frightened, hungry, and thirsty,
caged like animals.

This, too, I will remember...
The humiliation and sadness.
Cries of the children in the air,
death, destruction, hopelessness, and despair

This, too, I will remember...
Those who closed their eyes,
covered their ears,
and silenced their voices;
oblivious to the suffering and tears.

This, too, I will remember...
The ones who cared,
spoke out and shared
our suffering with others.

We will remember them as our
sisters and brothers...
All of this, I will remember...
Be it kindness
I will not forget
Kindness in return, you will get...
For those that heaped on us suffering and death
We will remember this until our last dying breath...
All of this we will always remember...

Kindness

A few years back, on a particularly bitter cold day, I was parked across the street from a soup kitchen in downtown Detroit, waiting for my son to get done with court.

While sitting in my truck, I ran the engine intermittently for warmth as I watched homeless people walking to and from the soup kitchen across the street, blowing on their hands. Many came out with cups of hot coffee, steam rising from them.

Being an avid coffee drinker, I really wanted a coffee, but there was nothing close by, and I did not want to give up the parking spot I had paid for, so I just put my head down, closed my eyes, and tried to get into the music blaring in my truck.

As I was about to doze off, I was startled by a tapping on my window. I lifted my head to see a homeless African American woman wrapped in rags, holding a cup of hot coffee. A warm smile emanated from her weathered face, a face that had endured too much suffering, as she motioned for me to open my window.

Not knowing what to expect, I put my window down halfway and said, "Hi, can I help you?"

She smiled again and said in a soft, gentle voice, "You look like you needed a coffee. I promise I did not drink from it. Here's some sugar and cream too."

I was at a loss for words as I took the paper cup from her weathered hands, and all I could muster was a weak "Thank you. God bless you."

She walked away, still smiling...

As I drank my coffee, I could not help thinking about the kindness that the homeless woman had shown me. One of the greatest cups of coffee I had ever had.

It might have been subpar coffee served in a soup kitchen, but it hit the spot, and that day didn't quite feel as cold as before.

Mint Tea

A Cup of Mint tea
Holds a special meaning for me

The flavor and fragrant smell
Triggers memories that I remember
rather well

Of mothers' beautiful garden in Palestine

Filled with beauty and sites, truly divine

The flowers, herbs, and vegetables...
a sight so great
From which I was torn away at the age
of eight

The plants of mint were special in many
ways
For they added an aroma that flavored
our lives in countless ways

The mint in my garden today
Originated from a sprig in my mothers
purse as a stowaway

So that each time I sip a cup of mint tea
The memory and flavor of my homeland
is right here with me…

A sip from a cup of mint tea
Is a sip of Palestine for me…

Aunt Jamila (Um Ali)

Dedicated to the memory of my aunt Jamila (Um Ali) Allah Yirhamah, who passed away today, 2-6-11.

I could not wait to get home yesterday. My wife had called me and told me that a package from Palestine had arrived. I relish these "care" packages from my mother and brother in Palestine. They usually send me, amongst other things, pure, cold-pressed, virgin olive oil. It cannot be brought anywhere in the world.

This special oil, you see, is by no means ordinary. It comes exclusively from my family's ancient olive orchards. Some of these trees are hundreds of years old and were planted by my ancestors, who had enjoyed their bounty for many years before me.

The reason I was excited was that I had also asked them to send a few packages of dried whole-leaf Za'atar (wild thyme that grows in the hills of Palestine) and, last but not least, some of Mother's famous cracked olives.

The cracked olives are also from our trees. They were hand-picked, cracked, and pickled by my mother's loving hands. My kids often tell me that no matter what their grandmother makes, it always tastes better than anything they have ever had.

My eldest son attributes this to the "special grandma hands" that prepare these foods.

Za'atar is a Palestinian stable. It is served on the side with meals and sometimes as a snack. The Za'atar is usually picked in springtime from the hills of Palestine. After drying, the Za'atar is then mixed with sumac and other spices, ground to a semi-powdery consistency, and the toasted sesame seeds are added. The ground mixture is then served with olive oil on the side.

The proper way to eat it is to dip a piece of bread in olive oil and then dip it into the Za'atar. The oil makes the Za'taar stick to the bread, adding to its delicious flavor. I cannot count how many breakfasts and midnight snacks I ate Za'atar.

My children today in America eat the Za'atar that grows in the hills of the land of my birth, just as their ancestors had done hundreds of years earlier in Palestine. In fact, the Zatar and olive oil they eat today come from Palestine exclusively. The hills and orchards of their ancestry still provide them with their favorite food. The thread continues.

Whole leaf Za'atar is very hard to come by here in the US. I have tried many times the small packages of "organic wild thyme" sold at obscene prices here in the US but to no avail. The taste does not even come close. The "zest" is missing.

That is why I was so excited. My mom, who lives in Palestine, makes some of the most delicious salads out of Za'atar. The taste of her salad is beyond description. When I returned to Palestine last June with my wife and kids, the first thing I asked my mother to make for me was breakfast that consisted of her famous Za'atar salad, cracked olives, and homemade cheese.

This, along with a pot of mint tea, was my dream meal.

Za'atar salad is made from fresh whole-leaf Za'atar, olive oil, salt, and freshly squeezed lemon juice from the lemon trees that grow just outside our window.

When I returned to Palestine in the spring of 2000, I could not contain my excitement. This was my first trip home to Palestine during the springtime. I had not experienced spring in Palestine since I left in 1969.

The hills that surround my village were ablaze with greenery and color. I was nostalgic for the days of my youth when I spent endless days playing and exploring the hills of my village.

I convinced my younger brother, my cousin (who was visiting from California), and a few friends to meet us and head for the hills to pick wild Za'atar (the wild variety has a bit more zest and flavor than other varieties).

We decided to make an afternoon of it. We packed homemade goat cheese, fresh sliced tomatoes, some nuts and seeds, a few sprigs of mint, a teapot, and a portable gas cooktop so that we could make mint tea on the hilltop.

Along the way to the hills, we stopped by my aunt's home, which is midway up the hill. We were surprised to find her baking fresh whole wheat bread in the taboon (a clay and earthen wood-fired oven whereby bread is baked over small, round, and smooth stones just as it had been for hundreds of years in the villages of Palestine.

She gave us a half dozen hot loaves of her famous bread (the likes of which I have yet to taste anywhere in the world). Armed with hot bread, we continued to the top of the hill.

Once we reached our destination, we spread out in our hunt for the elusive Za'atar plants that grow only during the spring in the hills of Palestine. When we had gathered enough Za'atar, we spread out a blanket, and our "picnic" started with the fresh Za'atar, hot fresh bread, and mint tea.

This was by far one of the highlights of my trip to Palestine. It conjured up memories of many years ago of olive harvests and the simple pleasures of life on one's land that the Fellah of Palestine had enjoyed. It was not hard to imagine this scene must have been played out countless times before by the people of Palestine. The attachment between the Palestinian people and their land is unparalleled.

As the sun began to set, bathing the entire village and the surrounding hills in their golden glow, I sat silent, sipping tea. My mind drifted to the Palestinian refugees who were forced off their lands and can only dream of this scene as they waste away in the miserable, squalid, and cramped refugee camps. These scenes are now no more than distant memories and the topics of countless stories told and retold to children who listen in wide-eyed awe.

I also could not help but think of the Jewish settlements that seemed to dwarf and, indeed, dominate the village of my birth. Every time I see them, it seems as if they have gotten bigger and moved closer.

These settlements do keep getting bigger and swallow more Palestinian land. They look like they are about to "pounce" on the villages below. Their domination of the Palestinian villages is a symbol of the occupation and what it seeks to accomplish. The aim is to dominate and subjugate the Palestinian people and their lands.

But as I look at the lone ancient olive tree that stands on the very top of the hill, as it has for hundreds more years than Israel has been a state, I am heartened. This tenacious windswept tree, which grows in the direction of the winds that have been buffeting it for hundreds of years, is still standing proud, much like the people who planted it and many more trees like it in Palestine. It has survived and thrived in very harsh and inhospitable conditions. So, too, will the people of Palestine.

The Legend of "Jaber Yassein"

"Jaber Yassein" was a name I heard quite a bit as a young child when I lived in our small village in Palestine. The name seemed to "come up" quite frequently, especially when we kids would intrude or quickly visit an adult conversation. The adults would be engaged in a conversation about a serious subject, and when we would pop in or stop to listen, the name "Jaber Yassein" would pop up out of nowhere, and the adults would either change the subject or stop and tell us to leave.

It seemed to me that "Jaber Yassein" was a very well-known and respected man because all the adults in our village knew him and spoke his name regularly. I even heard his name frequently uttered when the Israeli army would come into our village or when a stranger would come into our village and ask questions.

Yes, "Jaber Yassein" was indeed a very dark and mysterious man, and I had no idea who he was, what he looked like, what he did, where he lived, or if he was still alive. I was very curious about this man, as many children my age were, but no one would tell us anything about him. He remained a mystery to me. That is until I was eighteen.

In the summer of 1979, I traveled back home to Palestine for the first time since 1969, when I left at the age of eight. It had been ten years since I last saw my mother, who had been my life's focus, my inspiration, and my role model (she still is).

Shortly after my arrival, I sat down with my mother in the morning, and we enjoyed a cup of coffee — the first time for me as an "adult"—under the canopy of our 75-year-old grapevine that snaked its way around the staircase that led to the second-level veranda and dazzling bunches of golden grapes dangling above our heads.

I finally had the opportunity to ask my mother about this mythological figure, Jaber Yassein, who had puzzled me for nearly fourteen years. I had even heard his name mentioned a few times in America. It seemed to me that the only people who uttered this man's name were from our ancestral village of Beit Hanina. No one else seemed to know of him outside our village.

I looked my mother in the eye and asked her point-blank, "Who or what is Jaber Yassein?".

She looked at me for a moment and then let out a loud laugh. "Jaber Yassein?" she asked. "Why are you asking about him?"

Patiently, I spelled out my fascination and the curiosity bottled up inside of me for such a long time. I simply wanted to know who this man was and why his name was spoken so often by the elders of our village.

For the next hour or so, my mother told me the secret story of "Jaber Yassein ..."

It seems that sometime in the early 1900s, the people of Beit Hanina decided they should form a kind of "village watch" whereby armed men would take turns patrolling the village streets, especially at night.

These men were supposed to look out for strangers and thieves who liked to sneak into the villages and steal from them. They also feared the "watchmen" who would patrol the village, especially at night, and wanted to be able to identify friends from foes from a distance. They did not want to get up close to people without knowing whether they were from the village.

After much discussion, the people of Beit Hanina agreed that they would employ a "secret password" to be used exclusively among themselves. This password would enable anyone from the village to identify themselves to each other, especially at night, since Beit Hanina, like most rural Palestinian villages, had no electricity.

The password that the people of Beit Hanina agreed on was the nonexistent "Jaber Yassein." By uttering this name, people were allowed safe passage in and around the village.

And so, the legend of "Jaber Yassein" was born. The cries of "Who goes there?" would be met with an enthusiastic, "Jaber Yassein!"

The name soon became a codeword frequently used by the villagers of Beit Hanina, especially the elders. If they happened to be discussing something they did not want to share with outsiders or us kids, they would inject the name "Jaber Yassein" into the conversation, whereby everyone knew to change the subject or just end the conversation. What the codeword meant was widely understood, and it had many other uses besides what it was originally meant for.

If my mother had guests and could not talk on the phone, she would say "Jaber Yassein," and I would know what she meant by it. Also, if I slipped up and said something stupid or inappropriate in front of guests or strangers, all my mom had to do was say "Jabber Yassein." I would instinctively know to either shut up or change the subject entirely.

In the summer of 2002, while I was back home in Palestine with my wife and kids, my eldest son approached me and wanted to know who "Jaber Yassein" was. I asked him where he heard it, and he said that he heard his grandmother say the name to the taxi driver, also from Beit Hanina, as we were going through the Israel army checkpoint … The legend of "Jaber Yassein" lives on!

Covering Up Crimes

Approximately seventy years ago, the ethnic cleansing of Palestine commenced in earnest as more than 500 Palestinian villages were ethnically cleansed of their indigenous inhabitants, The Muslim and Christian Arabs, by the Zionist Colonial armed gangs and early adopters of systematic terrorism.

In November of 2016, forest fires erupted around the area just outside Jerusalem, burning thousands of trees non-native species of pine trees that were planted by the Zionists, with the financial backing of many Americans and Europeans who enthusiastically donated money to Jews and their Christian allies through the JNF (Jewish National Fund) and those ubiquitous "Blue Boxes" as they went from door to door, stationed themselves outside arenas, and placed them in local grocery stores to help "Redeem and Reclaim the Land of Israel" by "Planting a Tree in Israel."

What many of those who donated to this nefarious endeavor did not realize was that they were working hand in hand with war criminals by helping them cover up their crimes in Palestine.

As the Zionist terror gangs marched from village to village, they committed atrocities and ethnically cleansed villages by all means necessary, after which, as per the orders of Ben Gurion, all structures, fields, and orchards were reduced to dust to "erase them from the face of the earth" and ensure no return of their owners.

The Zionists chose fast-growing pine trees of European origin (just like themselves) to be planted over the destroyed villages and to ensure that the native vegetation would not reemerge because the shade and oils from the pine trees and their needles "sanitize" the soil, making it nearly impossible for any regrowth, turning the area into a "national forest" more suitable for the Swiss Alps than the arid climate of Palestine.

Last week, while hiking through the remains of the ethnically cleansed Palestinian village of Nataf, a rusted old key belonging to a Palestinian home was visible due to being "uncovered" as the fires cleansed the Zionist attempt at erasing the village and any evidence that it ever existed.

The key was found in what was once a courtyard on the side of the village road, and as I looked at the picture of that key, it stirred and moved me to tears. I could not help but think of the story that precious key, hidden for nearly seventy years under the lies of time, could tell.

I imagined a family fleeing their ancestral home in fear, children crying, leaving their life and belongings behind a "locked door," key in hand, believing that through that key, they would one day return "home."

Upon reaching the road, they were confronted by the Zionist gangs, stripped of what little belongings they had and in the process, dropping that precious key.

And so that key lay there waiting as the Zionists and their conspirators imported foreign trees and money to erase its existence and the story it had to tell, emerging only after a destructive and cleansing fire cleared away the seventy-year-old lies of Zionist myths and propaganda.

Below is a picture of that key, the village, and those dubious blue boxes that California Senator Kamala Harris bragged about as she went door to door to collect money to "plant a tree in Israel."

Unexpected Privilege

on April 1st, 1978, at the age of seventeen, I rode my bike to the Ambassador Bridge, hitched a ride across to Canada, and rode my bike approximately fifty miles to a small town called Erieau on the shore of Lake Erie. I lived there for five months—no one stopped me or asked me for identification on either side, which was good because I didn't have any on me.

Once there, in need of money and a place to stay, I passed a farmer on a tractor, struck up a conversation about hockey, and asked him if he was looking for help.

He asked me if I knew how to drive a tractor (I didn't), and I said, "Sure," even though I didn't even have a driver's license.

He hired me to drive a tractor and do chores on an onion farm for $15 a day (Canadian).

After securing a job, I rode past an older man working in his yard. I noticed He was struggling to get a ladder out of the back of his station wagon. I stopped and asked him if he needed a hand.

He said, "Why not..."

I carried the ladder into the garage of this cute cottage on Lake Erie. He offered me something to drink, and soon, I knew everything about this eighty-year-old retired auto worker from Detroit.

The cottage was his baby, but due to a bad heart requiring surgery, he and his wife (he had two daughters who lived out of state) would not be spending their usual summer at the cottage.

He told me the place needed some work, such as painting the exterior, staining the natural wood interior, etc.. And then, out of the blue, he asked me if I knew how to do those things.

I said, "Sure," even though I had never done them before.

Soon he offered to let me stay in this idyllic beachfront cottage in exchange for fixing it up and taking care of it. He also said I could use the boat if I liked to fish (a seventeen-year-old's dream).

I spent five awesome months driving a tractor, painting, cleaning, swimming, fishing, and having one hell of an improbable adventure, riding my Schwinn bike five miles into town for groceries and snacks. I even made friends with the neighbors who took a liking to this longhaired Palestinian Muslim teenager who blasted Led Zeppelin while working in shorts and no shirt, making me a few shades darker by the end of that beautiful summer.

I was blessed

Baby Blue Cadillac

In the summer of 1979, my late father (ay), who loved driving, buying, and selling cars, purchased a 1976 baby blue Cadillac El Dorado, the epitome of American luxury and status at the time.

He loved that car, but he also loved flipping cars even more, rarely keeping one for more than a year. He started going to the auto auctions back in 1972, going on a weekly basis, buying whatever caught his eye on a spur of the moment. I never knew what car he was going to be driving back when he left that day. It was an "adventure" to say the least.

Back to that baby blue Cadillac. One morning my dad handed me the keys and instructed me to take it to the car wash, clean it inside and out, and drive it to the Beit Hanina Social Club in Dearborn's Southend and wait for him because he had agreed to sell it to a Lebanese guy for a nice profit and the guy was coming with the cash to pick it up.

I was 18 years old, and excited to be driving such an amazingly luxurious car. It was big, heavy, and over the top in features for it's day. Pure Detroit automotive excellence. I drove it to the car wash, meticulously cleaning it as many admirers looked on and complemented on my "nice ride". I just soaked it in and turned up the volume on my Led Zeppelin 8-Track tape for the added "cool factor"...I was "the man"...

After hand drying the shiny clean car, I jumped in, rolled down the windows, and headed down Vernor Avenue towards my destination, music blasting at ear splitting level. The sun was shining and as drove along, I was getting many admiring looks, especially from the opposite sex. I was young, shoulder length hair blowing in wind, great music, and a cool car, the perfect "chick magnet" if there ever was one.

While driving down that busy avenue, my eyes were all over the place, checking out the opposite sex that was checking me out, when suddenly, the red Dodge van in front me stopped, and me paying attention to everything but what was in front me, hit my brakes, but too little too late. Did I mention that the car I was driving was heavier than a tank? I slammed into the rear end of the van, causing extensive damage to rear end of the van, and of course to that beautiful, distinct, heavily chromed front end.

The cops came, issued me a ticket for following too close and causing an accident, and I resumed my trip, in silence, fear and dread. Long gone was that swagger as fear set in. All I could think about was the old man waiting to show off his Cadillac...

I slowly limped in to the parking lot and parked the car where the front wouldn't be visible. My dad arrived, took the keys and went to look see if had done a good job in cleaning it. I stayed behind in the company of some elders playing cards, seeking safety and thinking to myself that he wouldn't dare shoot me with so many witnesses around. When he got to the car you could hear him yelling in the next county. I think he exhausted every bad word in English, Arabic, and Spanish (he was fluent) that day. The sale was off! He was beyond mad and my only saving grace was the fact that I was scheduled to fly back home to Palestine the next day for the first time since I left 10 years earlier...The 45 days I was gone was almost sufficient enough for him to cool down...Almost

A Haunting Memory

From 1969 to 2000, I was haunted by a vague memory of myself, extremely young, sitting atop a round, grated cover with a faint light shining below. This memory would appear, disappear, and reappear and had me flummoxed for years until one day in April of 2000.

After taking my late mother (Ay) to make Hajj (The Pilgrimage to Mecca), I went back with her to Palestine to complete my Hajj in Al-Quds (Jerusalem).

While home, we decided to go to Al-Khalil (Hebron) and pray at the Ibrahimi Mosque. As soon as we entered, I said a special prayer for the Muslim worshipers Baruch Goldstein massacred in cold blood.

When I entered the tomb area of the Prophet Abraham, there it was, the round metal grate covering that had haunted me for years!

I called my mother over and told her of my recurring dream/memory. .She gave me a look of utter disbelief!

My mother said, "But you were so young!"

She then explained that she had brought me to this very Mosque when I was two years old in 1962 and sat me on that round metal grate, which led down to the tomb of the Prophet Abraham, and that light? That was the oil lamps that are kept burning.

I finally had my answer, and just like that, I no longer had those dreams...Allah Akbar!

Teaching Hatred

Not a day goes by without having to read or listen to someone from the 'Israel right or wrong camp' spin tales about Palestinians teaching their children to 'hate.' From those aspiring higher public office, such as Hillary Clinton, to hatemongering lunatics, such as Pat Robertson and Daniel Pipes, they do not miss an opportunity to propagate this lie in the hopes of portraying Palestinian parents and society as a whole as 'lesser' human beings, unfit to raise their children 'properly.'

Although this myth about Palestinian parents and their children has been debunked countless times by many experts, including Israeli academics and journalists in the Hebrew press, this has not stopped those who seek to demonize the Palestinians at every turn in their endless campaign to brainwash the American public so that Israel's nefarious actions and policies against the much-maligned and brutalized Palestinian people can be dismissed or 'excused,' because, after all, in their eyes, Palestinians and their children couldn't possibly be regarded as equally 'human.'

As a child growing up in Palestine, where we had no television or, for that matter, any electricity, the first time I was ever exposed to the Star of David was when I saw it painted on the gleaming metallic bodies of the Fantom jet fighters flying low overhead as they bombed and strafed the outskirts of our village and nearly massacred us as we huddled along with twenty others, escaping mere minutes a missile from one the jets that destroyed the cave where we sought refuge.

The first Jew I had ever seen in my life was an alien-looking figure who stood atop a tank—which also had the Star of David painted on it—pointing a gun at my mother and shouting at us in a language I had never before heard. The first Jew I had ever seen close-up, was also pointing a gun at me, even though I was a mere child of six.

Many times during the early period of Israel's occupation of my homeland, the only Jews that I encountered were Israeli soldiers who marched into our village, forcing every male aged twelve to seventy-five to go out onto the village's open fields and sit under the brutal summer sun for hours, with little regard for their safety and well being.

These soldiers were also the ones who clamped daily curfews on our villages and, in one night, while we were confined to our homes, came into our village and killed every dog they could find. For many days after this dastardly act, the stench of the decaying flesh permeated throughout the village.

On more than one occasion, I witnessed Jewish soldiers physically and verbally abusing Palestinian men, women, and children. Some of these soldiers seemed to relish the power their guns and uniforms gave them, showing a sadistic zeal for their 'work.'

Countless Palestinian children had their very first or only encounters with Jews as I had, whether in Palestine or the refugee camps of Lebanon and elsewhere. The 'Jewish' face of Israel, to us, manifested itself in the persona of the Israeli soldier.

By contrast, the first Christian I had ever encountered looked and sounded just like me, a native Palestinian who did not present a threat to me nor my family and who shared our language, customs, food, and dress.

Thus, my perception of Jews was profoundly influenced by the experiences of my encounters with Israeli soldiers. I was one of the 'lucky ones' because thousands of other Palestinian children were forever scarred as they had to witness the killings, beatings, midnight raids, humiliations, and imprisonment of their fathers, siblings, and other loved ones by the Israelis.

The Star of David was not a religious symbol to me and other Palestinians. It was a symbol of oppression and fear, for it was painted on the side of the Israeli army's machines of death.

It was not until I came to America that I met a Jew who did not seem to threaten me and who looked and acted 'normal,' like everyone around him. Since then, I have come to meet and befriend many Jews in America and elsewhere, showing me a 'different' side of Jews I had no idea existed.

My children, on the other hand, were born and raised in the United States and had gotten to meet and know many of my Jewish friends. Although they knew much about what the Israelis were doing to our people, they didn't look at Jews in this country any differently than any other Americans.

It wasn't until the summer of 2003 that my children began to see Jews in a different light. Standing in the hot summer sun at the Israeli checkpoints, they were witness to Israeli oppression and cruelty firsthand, staring in shock as a young Palestinian father was sat upon and beaten by Israeli soldiers for having the 'audacity' to complain because his pregnant wife and two young children had to stand in the sweltering heat for hours at the Qalandia Checkpoint on their way home.

I will never forget the shock on my children's faces as I tried to help the young father up after he was beaten in front of his wife and young children.

More than anything else, it is the Israelis themselves who are having the greatest influence on the youths of Palestine. By their words and deeds, they are the ones who are teaching the Palestinian children to hate because, as we all know, experience is the greatest 'teacher' of them all, and the Israelis are doing one hell of a job 'teaching' it.

The American poet Auden said it best:

I and the public know what all school children learn, those to whom evil is done do evil in return...

At Gunpoint

In the spring of 2012, I decided to take my father (AY) and my boys to the small neighborhood grocery store my dad owned in Detroit from 1970-78. My children had grown up with my tales of working with my father from the age of nine (I used to stand on a milk crate to reach the cash register to ring people up) until seventeen at this store, which was once a pharmacy from the 1930s until 1969. Of course, the area had changed dramatically from when we owned it, with bulletproof glass enveloping the counters.

When we owned it, it was the prototypical neighborhood store where families were routinely extended credit and paid when they could. My father knew everyone in the neighborhood, and they knew him (and, of course, me).

Our customer base was predominately of Eastern European origin (Polish). We sold a Polish-language newspaper and even printed the calendars we passed out at Christmas in Polish and English.

The customers called my father "Danny," and I eventually convinced him to change the store's name to "Danny's Corner" because the store was on the corner of Michigan and Livernois.

We lived above the store for a while, just my dad and me, for a few years before he sold it to a couple of Chaldean brothers.

Although I had many great memories of that store and the customers, I was held up at gunpoint once when I was thirteen and on another occasion after closing the store on a Sunday night (I was fourteen at the time).

I wanted to walk down to the Burger King store about four blocks away. As I passed the dark alley, I was accosted by a one-armed man with a gun. He stuck the gun between my eyes and ordered me into the dark-lit alley. Once out of sight, he cocked the revolver and explained that he was going to kill me. I was so terrified that tears rolld down my face.

I asked him, "Why? What did I do to you?"

He said, "Nothing! It's something that I have to do."

All I could see was the barrel of that gun, which looked as big as a cannon mere inches from my forehead.

As he pushed me deeper into the back of the building, near a large dumpster, and me begging through my tears for him to let me go, I heard sirens and speeding police cars flying by us, which distracted him momentarily, allowing me to run, and *run* I did.

I ran as fast as my legs could move, not slowing down for anything, crossing streets with reckless abandon, not feeling the pavement under my feet. I must have ran a mile or more before I stopped to look back.

Later I discovered that the one-armed man was found dead by his wife in the morning. He was a Viet Nam vet who had mental issues after losing his arm and had killed himself that night.

Life is Beautiful

A couple of days ago, I woke in the middle of the night to terrible pains in my upper stomach. I had forgotten to take my daily dose of medicine, and now I had to pay the price.

The pains are such that it hurts more when I lay down. The only way to find relief was to stand up and walk. The pains usually go through a stage, lasting anywhere from two to three hours, and always occur in the middle of the night. So I paced back and forth in the family room at 3 AM.

I went downstairs because I didn't want to wake my wife and children, who were sound asleep. While I continued to pace, trying to seek comfort from the pain, I turned on the TV.

As I flipped through the endless channels and their irritable infomercials, I stumbled across the late showing of one of my favorite films, Life Is Beautiful. I had seen this compelling and moving film, which garnered a few Academy Awards more than once.

I happened to switch on the show at the point in the film where the man and his son are being transported to the concentration camp. There and then, I stopped pacing and started watching the movie while standing up, for sitting aggravated my pains.

The movie ended at around 4:30 am, and I was still standing and watching. I was so engrossed in the film and its emotional message about life that I did not notice that my pains had ceased.

I was teary-eyed as usual by the time the boy was reunited with his mother in the climactic ending of the movie. The message and story of this magnificently portrayed human drama never loses its power, no matter how many times I have seen it. The story of a man trying to carry on for the sake of his son in the midst of the most horrible of conditions imaginable resonates deeply with me as a Palestinian and, more importantly, as a human being.

The reason I connect with this film is not because the victims are Jews but because they are human beings. The very act of a parent trying to shield and spare his child from certain harm and man's inhumanity is a universal message that transcends all ethnic and religious lines, whether the setting is in the concentration camps of the Nazis, or the impoverished land of Gaza.

There is a sanctity to life in all of its forms. No label must be allowed to dull our senses and make the destruction of life somehow right, permissible. For far too long, we have lived with the labels that paint conflicts as US versus *them*.

We attach labels to human beings to sap their very humanity from them and to facilitate their oppression, abuse, and death. The child becomes something less when he is perceived as having the opportunity to grow up and become one of *them*. His death is somehow dismissed as having attained the act of legitimacy. He was not a child but a future one of *them*.

The death of innocents is spun in so many ways that after a while, we all become criminals. There are no innocents if one is to believe the spin. The value of human life is cheapened. What makes one life more valuable than the next? Don't we all have dreams and aspirations for our people and children? My dreams for my children's future and that of my grandchildren are not of pain and suffering. I dream of a peaceful life and future for my grandchildren to realize their full potential as human beings. I did not have children to see them suffer or inflict suffering on others.

Their race and or religion should not measure the value and importance of a human life. The humble peasant trying to earn a living in the besieged Strip of Gaza is just as important as the one who sits in an air-conditioned office and rarely are their hands dirty. Both are working for basically the same thing. They are trying, to the best of their abilities and resources, to provide for their families. Both harbor dreams and ambitions that differ only in their scope and chances of attaining them.

In the end, we must realize that life is a sacred and precious thing. Whether one resides in gleaming towers that reach for the heavens, in a mud hut, or in the teeming poverty of a Palestinian refugee camp, Life is indeed *beautiful*.

A Sign of Respect

In October of 2007, my mother (AY) became ill and was hospitalized. I flew back home in a hurry via Lufthansa Airlines. My connecting flight on a 747 from Frankfurt to Tel Aviv was solidly booked (overwhelming Jewish). I got on the plane and headed to my seat. My seat was an aisle seat, which I had requested, and when I went to sit down, I discovered that an elderly Jewish woman was already there, and next to her was a religious-looking man in his seventies.

When I approached my seat, the man stood and objected, saying, "No! No!"

Now, knowing what I knew of religious Jews, he didn't want a man sitting next to his wife, and being a Muslim, I understood, so out of respect, I offered to sit in the window seat, letting the husband be a "buffer" between me and his wife.

When I sat down, he spoke to me in broken English, asking me my name and where I was headed.

I said, "Jerusalem, Palestine, the city of my birth."

To my surprise, he said in perfect Arabic, "I, too, was born in Al Quds."

After getting to know one another, I found out he emigrated to Australia in the late '60s and is a chief Rabbi there.

I told him I was heading to see my sick mother, and he promised he would pray for her all along the flight and as soon as he set foot in Jerusalem.

Meanwhile, as more people boarded, an Orthodox Jewish family made their way to the seats in front of us, the wife and kids in the row in front, and the father had the seat I was sitting in. To make things worse, he made a fuss and refused to sit elsewhere, saying he wanted to be with his family. Even the Rabbi's pleas fell on deaf ears. The man called the flight crew and demanded his seat!

The Rabbi and his wife became distraught, and that was when I got up and asked the flight crew to find me a seat, any seat so that the Rabbi and his wife could stay together.

When they finally found me a seat, and I got up to leave, the Rabbi also got up, and when I stuck out my hand to shake his goodbye, he grabbed my hand and *kissed* it *twice* in front of a plane full of Jews headed to Israel.

He hugged me and, in Arabic, said, "Thank you, my dear brother!"

You could hear a pin drop as all the Jews around us looked on in amazement.

We landed at Ben Gurion Airport, and I was being led away for "further questioning," the rabbi ran up to me, took my hand, kissed it, and said, "What are you doing to my *brother*?"

He grabbed me and shepherded me through.

Needless to say, the Airport Security let me go. One of the only times I can recall not having to spend four to five hours at "security." Note: In our culture, kissing a person's hand is the ultimate show of respect.

Seedless Fruit...

Seedless fruit! The perversity of it all...

On the one hand, we want to eat and enjoy the taste of grapes. On the other hand, we do not want the nuisance of having to deal with the seeds. Fruits, yes; seeds, no.

Without the seeds, there would never be grapes. They are viewed as an obstacle to our unfettered enjoyment of the fruit, and life would be better without them. We look for ways to remove what we perceive as the obstacle to our full and unhindered enjoyment of that fruit.

Although the first seedless grapes were a genetic mistake by Mother Nature, we seized upon that. Just as some humans are infertile and cannot reproduce, so too it goes for plants and animals. The seedless grapes were an aberration, not the norm. Humans decided they preferred these fruits without their seeds.

Plants, unlike humans, can be reproduced by the use of cuttings. A small branch is cut and placed in a rooting compound until roots develop and then planted in the soil.

This works for almost all species of plants. The only exception is the citrus plants. This way, we can control what we want to grow, where, and whether we would allow the species to propagate. This is ideal for humans, but I am not sure about the plants. I don't think this is what Mother Nature had intended.

This brings me to draw this analogy of our history as Palestinians: we are the seeds of the fruit that grows on the trees in the fertile Palestine soil. The fruit of Palestine would have never been if it weren't for the seeds. Some would prefer that the Palestinian fruit become "seedless." This way, it could be developed, settled, and "enjoyed" fully without regard to the nuisance of its seeds.

The Zionists dreamed of a seedless fruit. They knew full well that this type of plant cannot propagate with cuttings. The seeds are essential for the plant to survive, just like the citrus trees that are abundant in Palestine.

The Zionists need to understand that the Palestinian fruit will never become "seedless." the fruit of Palestine will always have seeds, and no amount of "engineering" will ever change that...

Friendship and Trust

My late mother (ay) used to say, "Smile in my presence, and I'm indebted to you. Give me a glass of water when I'm thirsty, and I will never forget."

Throughout my life, God blessed me with the kindness of strangers, most of whom were neither Arab nor Muslim. I would be remiss for not acknowledging them, their kindness, and generosity.

From the German Catholic lady who took on the role of "surrogate mother" to me early on, respecting my heritage and beliefs, to the Irish Catholic school teacher who saw something special in me and pushed me hard to be the best, to the Canadian farmers who treated me as a son, to the small Northern Michigan farming community of Marlette who accepted me as one their own, when I was probably the only Arab/Muslim they ever met, to the Jewish electronics store owner I befriended and became very close friends with who supported me when I needed it most, to the Christian sports dealer who a few months after meeting me, extended his friendship and a line of credit in the hundreds of thousands of dollars based on nothing more than a handshake...

Yes, I've been blessed beyond my wildest dreams, and I want to thank God for placing these wonderful people into my life, some of whom have passed away while others are still here, and I'm proud to call them my friends in the truest sense of the word.

Thank you to all the fine folks in Marlette and my classmates from the class of 1979, to Bernard Kaselemas, who has heard just about every inappropriate Jewish joke from me (get well, my friend), and my old friends Richard Dvorsky Joan Dvorsky...I love you all.

Made in the USA
Monee, IL
16 March 2024

54645248R00094